EIR (ISSN 0273-6314) *is published weekly (50 issues), by EIR News Service, Inc., P.O. Box 17390, Washington, D.C. 20041-0390. (703) 297-8434*

European Headquarters: E.I.R. GmbH, Postfach Bahnstrasse 9a, D-65205, Wiesbaden, Germany
Tel: 49-611-73650
Homepage: http://www.eir.de
e-mail: info@eir.de
Director: Georg Neudecker

Montreal, Canada: 514-461-1557
eir@eircanada.ca

Denmark: EIR - Danmark, Sankt Knuds Vej 11, basement left, DK-1903 Frederiksberg, Denmark.
Tel.: +45 35 43 60 40, Fax: +45 35 43 87 57. e-mail: eirdk@hotmail.com.

Mexico City: EIR, Sor Juana Inés de la Cruz 242-2 Col. Agricultura C.P. 11360
Delegación M. Hidalgo, México D.F.
Tel. (5525) 5318-2301
eirmexico@gmail.com

From Moscow, Helga Zepp-LaRouche Calls for a New Bretton-Woods Conference

EIR Contents

www.larouchepub.com Volume 45, Number 44, November 2, 2018

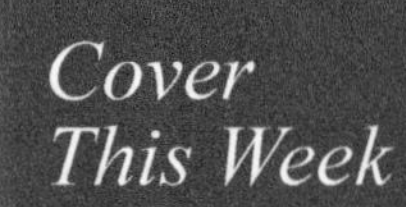

Moscow at night.

cc/Oleg Tokarev

**FROM MOSCOW,
HELGA ZEPP-LAROUCHE CALLS FOR A
NEW BRETTON-WOODS CONFERENCE**

A Community of Mankind's Shared Future: Strategic Perspective of China to 2050

by Helga Zepp-LaRouche

This is the presentation, as prepared in advance of delivery, by Mrs. LaRouche in Moscow to the 23rd International Academic Conference of the Institute of Far Eastern Studies of the Russian Academy of Sciences (RAS), Academic Council for Comprehensive Studies of Contemporary China, "China, Chinese Civilization and the World: Past, Present, and Future," which took place on October 24 and 25.

Lyndon LaRouche was a featured speaker at an RAS conference in 2003 on "China in the 21st Century: Chances and Challenges of Globalization." That conference was the 14th International Conference on "China, Chinese Civilization and the World: Past, Present and Future."

Schiller Institute

Helga Zepp-LaRouche, Founder and President of the Schiller Institute.

Oct. 26—The big question which should concern all thinking human beings on this planet, is essentially the same as that which was hotly debated in the young American republic as reported in the *Federalist Papers*, "Is human society capable of an efficient form of self-government?" Only this time it is not a question for just one nation; it concerns all of humanity and the need for a new paradigm in the world order.

Tensions in a world plagued by multiple crises seem to be increasing towards a breaking point: the danger of a new—this time systemic—financial crash of the transatlantic financial system, an unprecedented polarization inside the United States around the ongoing coup attempt against the President of the United States, false-flag operations, Goebbels-like deception operations against entire populations, drug epidemics which are a new form of Opium Wars, the global migration crisis, terrorism and Nazism, an increase of centrifugal forces in the European Union, the re-emergence of aggressive, geopolitically motivated efforts to defend an order that no longer exists—just to list some of the challenges. The world is in disorder.

In light of such a complex and seemingly completely disunited world, how realistic then is the perspective laid out at the 19th National Congress of the CPC by Chinese President Xi Jinping, where he defined the goal for China to become a "strong, democratic, culturally advanced, harmonious, and beautiful," fully modernized country by the year 2050, and even spoke at some point of the building of a "beautiful world" for all nations to participate in?

If one looks at the crises and challenges listed above as unrelated individual problems, one ends up in a "bad infinity," where the solution to many of them seems impossible. But if one recognizes that all of these problems have common threads, in that they are the derivatives of the old paradigm of an epoch going under, one can find the solution by being informed by the principles of the new epoch.

Two Game-Changing Pathways

There are two "game-changing" topics, which in the near future, create totally opposite pathways for mankind. The first one concerns the monumental battle being fought out now in the United States. The coup attempt against President Trump may be successful and he is driven out of office one way or the other. Or, if the collusion of the heads of intelligence agencies of the Obama administration with the British intelligence services (GCHQ and MI6) in orchestrating "Russiagate" against Trump—to prevent him from realizing his intention to put the relationship between the United States and Russia on a good basis—will lead to the criminal prosecution of the perpetrators.

Were the Democrats to win the House of Representatives in the midterm elections, they will try to bury the ongoing investigations in the Congress, and the confrontationist policies we have seen in the sanctions against Russia, the trade war against China, and the recent speech by Vice President Pence, will be escalated instantly. If Trump can consolidate his position, despite the many hawkish tones coming from the United States now, there does exist the potential that he will be able, in the second half of his first term, to improve relations with Russia and return to his initial positive attitude towards China.

The second, related game-changing issue is whether we fall into the "Thucydides Trap" or escape it. Let us look at a perspective to overcome the Thucydides Trap, the apparent conflict between the power dominating the world up to now, the United States, and the rising power, China, by defining a solution which goes way beyond the bilateral situation of the two, and which addresses the existential dangers for *all* nations, thus shifting the level of discussion and thinking to a higher plateau.

Helga Zepp-LaRouche at the 23rd International Academic Conference of the Russian Academy of Sciences Institute of Far Eastern Studies, Moscow, Russia, Oct. 24, 2018.

Vice President Mike Pence slams China at the Hudson Institute in Washington, D.C. on Oct. 14, 2018.

A New Bretton Woods Monetary System

My husband Lyndon LaRouche's proposal of several years ago is still valid: The four most powerful nations in the world—the United States, Russia, China and India—supported by other nations, Japan, South Korea and others—must set up in the short term a New Bretton Woods system to avoid the potentially devastating consequences of an uncontrolled financial collapse. This new international credit system must correct the flaws of the old Bretton Woods system, which was not realized as President Franklin Delano Roosevelt intended, but was corrupted by the influence of Churchill and Truman. It must guarantee the unconditional sovereignty of each and all nation-states participating in it, and it must promote their unlimited opportunities to participate in the benefits of scientific and technological progress to the mutual benefit of each and all.

This New Bretton Woods system must have as its most important feature a profound change in the monetary, economic and political relations among the dominant powers and the so-called developing nations. Unless the inequities lingering in the aftermath of modern colonialism are progressively remedied, neither can there be peace, nor can such challenges as the migration crisis or terrorism be overcome.

The Belt and Road Initiative

The basic conception for such a new credit and economic system already exists in principle in the Belt and Road policy of President Xi Jinping. In the five years of its existence it has created an unprecedented dynamic of hope and optimism among the approximately 100 countries participating in it and, given its rate of progress in such a short time, it is obvious that the goal defined by President Xi Jinping of a "beautiful world" by 2050 for all of humanity is absolutely achievable.

The new set of international relations required for the New Paradigm is already in the process of being built. The increasing integration of the Belt and Road Initiative, the Shanghai Cooperation Organization, the Eurasian Economic Union, and the Global South organizations, is progressing successfully and is already creating completely new strategic alliances for the mutual benefit of all participating in them. The "Spirit of the New Silk Road" has caught on in most countries of Asia and Latin America, and is providing the gift of hope, for the first time in centuries, to Africa, which President Xi has called the continent with the greatest development potential.

President Putin has promised in this context to "light up" the continent of Africa by providing it with nuclear technology. Many are now speaking of "Africa, the new China with African characteristics"! And despite the reluctance of the European Union and the present Berlin government, there is an increasing number of people in Europe who want their nations to be fully integrated into the New Silk Road, as shown in the 16+1 group [16 Central and Eastern European Countries plus China], as well as in Spain, Portugal, Switzerland, Netherlands, Belgium, and especially Austria and Italy.

The biggest, and unavoidable challenge, however, will be to find a solution which includes the United States. Given the level of militarization of the United States, both in terms of its armed forces as well as the arming of the population domestically, the chance, that the United States might disintegrate or accept being excluded from an alternative world system, as peacefully as it happened with the end of the Soviet Union is probably tending towards zero. The military policy of President Putin, announced on March 1, regarding Russian military science and the strategic alliance between Russia and China, shows Russian and Chinese clarity on this. So, if the Thucydides Trap is to be avoided, there has to be a design of a solution which integrates the United States in a higher order of organization of the world order.

A Community of Shared Future for Mankind

The common political platform offered must be conceptualized from the standpoint of what Nikolaus Kusansky [Nicholas of Cusa] defined as a completely new form of thinking, his famous *coincidentia opposi-*

Xinhua/Ju Peng

Chinese President Xi Jinping.

kremlin.ru

Russian President Vladimir Putin.

torum, the One, which has a higher order of reality than the Many. This is already implicit in President Xi Jinping's conception of the "shared community for the common future of Mankind."

Rather than approaching the question of the new set of relations among the nations of the world from the standpoint of proceeding from the status quo, the vision of the human species growing into adulthood in 50 or 100 years from now must include a set of concrete policy cooperation proposals. By that time, according to the scientific theory of Vladimir Vernadsky, the Noösphere will have advanced its dominance over the Biosphere qualitatively and new generations of scientists and classical artists will communicate with each other based on the search for new physical and artistic principles.

Rocket scientist and space pioneer Krafft Ehricke (left) shows his design of an orbital hospital to CBS-TV anchorman Walter Cronkite, Sept. 26, 1966.

As the German rocket scientist and space visionary Krafft Ehricke elaborated, the extension of infrastructure into first nearby space—as a precondition for interstellar space travel—is the necessary next level of the evolution of the human species. As the collaboration on the International Space Station and as the eye-opening findings of the Hubble Space Telescope have demonstrated, the emphasis on Mankind as a space-faring species completely changes the sense of identity of all astronauts, engineers and scientists involved. It has also completely replaced the notion that we are living in an Earth-bound system—where opposing geopolitical interests have to quarrel about limited resources—with the idea that mankind has just begun to take the very first baby steps into a universe in which there are an estimated two trillion galaxies.

The Chinese space program will soon provide another unprecedented game-changer by leading the world into a new scientific and industrial revolution. The ongoing Chang'e lunar missions include an ambitious program to bring back helium-3 from the Moon as fuel for controlled thermonuclear fusion on Earth. Once the human species can control thermonuclear fusion, we will have energy and raw materials security for the all Humankind for the foreseeable future.

Going in the same direction, the Chandrayaan-2 mission of the Indian Space Research Organization (ISRO) will analyze the lunar crust for traces of water and helium-3. President Trump declared manned space travel, the return to the Moon, and missions to Mars and "worlds far away," to be a national mission again. These, and related missions by the other space-faring nations, will not only benefit the countries involved, but all of Mankind.

Space science will transform every aspect of life on Earth, as the same general technologies and approaches to create habitable conditions in "wastelands" on the Earth, as with Umka, the Russian city planned for the Arctic, will be used to create villages on the Moon. Space technology will completely revolutionize the access to advanced medical care everywhere on Earth. Agriculture will benefit from many aspects of space research. The combination of a fusion economy and the industrialization of the Moon, as the next steps in an unlimited process of Mankind's continued mastery of the laws of the universe, will mean an entirely new economic platform in the sense defined by Lyndon LaRouche.

The Chandrayaan-2 mission will analyze the lunar crust for traces of water and helium-3.

If the many human beings in distress in the world—be it fleeing as a refugee from the scourges of poverty and war, or seeing society falling apart with an increase of violence, alcoholism, drug abuse or depression, or any other expression of desperation—can be brought to know about the immediate potentials for a breakthrough to a new era of Mankind, the New Silk Road Spirit will catch on and become the beacon of hope for all.

Such an ordering principle for our disunited world of today can become the basis for joint leadership by the presidents of China, Russia, India and the United States.

The Phenomenal Development of Xinjiang, and the Feudal Lords of London Who Want to Stop It

by Mike Billington

Oct. 29—The vast Chinese region of Xinjiang (Xinjiang Uyghur Autonomous Region) is the hub for the most ambitious global undertaking in modern history, or perhaps in all of history—the New Silk Road Economic Belt. When Xi Jinping announced the launching of this New Silk Road in Kazakhstan in Sept. 2013 (along with the 21st Century Maritime Silk Road, announced in Indonesia in Oct. 2013), the idea had already been percolating across Eurasia—starting with the fall of the Soviet Union, when Lyndon and Helga LaRouche posed the New Silk Road as a basis for ending geopolitics, bringing East and West together through joint development and cultural exchanges.

Change has been rapid. In 2017, more than 700 trains traveled through Xinjiang on the way to Europe, a number which is expected to reach 1,400 in 2018. The pace of development within Xinjiang itself is among the highest in all of China, reaching 7.6% in GDP growth in 2017. Growth in fixed assets reached 20% last year, with $70 billion allocated for infrastructure construction for 2018, including expansion of the Urumqi airport and new road and rail development across the region.

Yet, as anyone reading the Western press will be aware, over the past year a vast campaign to demonize China has been launched by the British and American imperial interests, accusing China of military aggression, labeling the Belt and Road Initiative an imperialist trick to entrap target nations in debt, and even claiming that China intends to replace the United States as a world hegemon. A major aspect of this campaign is

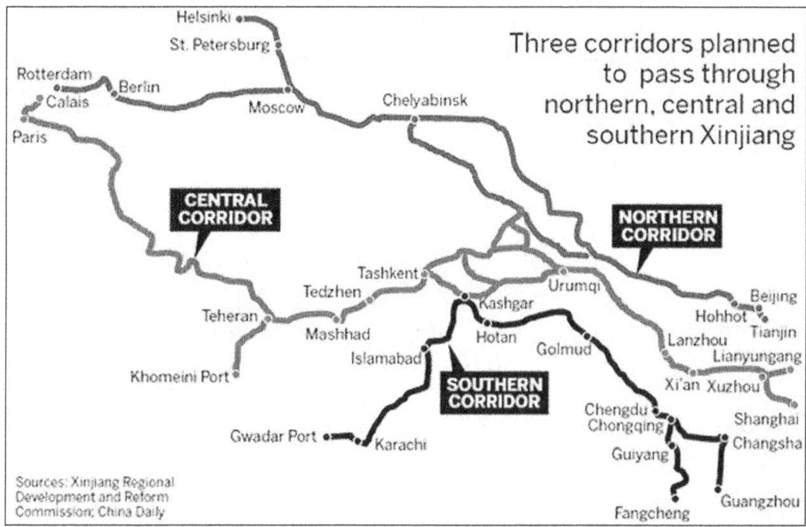

aimed at Xinjiang, fueled by the same "regime change" forces that gave us "color revolutions" around the world over the past decades, who are now attempting to mobilize international condemnation of China's supposed suppression of the human rights of the indigenous Uyghur population in Xinjiang—the Turkic Islamic people who make up about half of the mixed ethnicities in the region.

This is not new—the World Uyghur Congress was founded in 2004 in Germany, calling for independence of "East Turkestan" (a former name of the region), accusing China of "colonizing" the region and suppressing the Uyghur people. Not surprisingly, the World Uyghur Congress office in Washington has been shared with the Tibetan Centre for Human Rights and Democracy—both financed and supported by the National Endowment for Democracy, the primary color revolution institution in the United States, funded by the U.S. Government and the various George Soros NGOs.

These "Project Democracy" organizations essentially ignore the reality that the Uyghur population has been heavily targeted by the Wahhabi terrorist networks from Saudi Arabia, with many Uyghurs trained by Saudi and Pakistani terrorist networks. While acknowledging that there were a large number of terrorist attacks in Xinjiang since 2009 against Chinese police and common citizens of Han ethnicity, and even terrorist attacks by Uyghurs in Beijing and in Central Asian nations, these attacks are described as local phenomena driven by the repression of Uyghur rights. With an estimated 10,000 Uyghurs having joined the al Qaeda/al Nusra/ISIS terrorist forces in Syria, and many expected to return to Xinjiang now that they have been defeated in Syria, such arguments are no longer justified.

The Truth About 'Re-education' Camps

The current round of attacks on China's policies in Xinjiang center on the accusation that China has establish huge "re-education" facilities where tens of thousands (some claim millions) of Uyghurs have been sent for "brainwashing." BBC, in classic imperial fashion, issued a video titled "China's Hidden Camps," claiming to have used stealth to film the camps and interview "victims." In fact, the video makes many claims, but it is obvious that the BBC crew was allowed into Xinjiang; was allowed to drive around, to film the buildings they claim are internment camps; and was allowed to talk to people, although they were under observation by the police.

China does not deny the camps, reporting that people who have committed minor crimes under the influence of Islamic extremists have been sent to the camps for periods ranging from a few months to two years, where they receive vocational training, lessons in Mandarin, and classes to address the dangers and criminality of the extremist cults.

While the primary approach to ending the influence of the terrorists is the provision of a proper livelihood, which is the most fundamental human right, the government emphasizes that the security of the majority of the Uyghur population, and all other residents of Xinjiang, must be protected from terrorism by means other than conducting military operations against the terrorist cells.

While there are certain to be some excessive actions and some mistakes in the process, any sane view of the situation would encourage the effort to prevent the kinds of terrorist destabilizations and massive killing seen in the Arab world as a result of the "color revolutions" there, all openly financed and supported by the same "project democracy" operations in the United States and the UK that are now ranting against China.

The claims that Islam has been banned, that the use of the Uyghur language has been banned in education, and similar accusations in the western press are simply lies. There are 20 million Muslims in China, with about half of Uyghur ethnicity in Xinjiang. There are 57,000 Islamic clerics in China, and 39,000 mosques, 25,000 of them in Xinjiang, many associated with Islamic schools. The government openly says that all religions were severely persecuted in the first decades after the 1949 Revolution, but that it began to be reversed in 1978 after the death of Mao Zedong and the fall of the Gang of Four.

China released a White Paper this year titled "China's Policies and Practices on Protecting Freedom of Religious Belief," which encourages ties with foreign religious institutions, but forbids efforts to "interfere in China's religious affairs" or "subvert the Chinese government and socialist system under the guise of religion." Given the training of terrorists through the international Islamic networks, this proviso is to be expected. The document reports full protection for Muslim customs "regarding food and drink, clothing, festivals, marriages and funerals."

Real Development in Xinjiang

The phenomenal pace of development in Xinjiang in shown in the rate of growth both in the GDP of the region and the growth in the average wage over the past 20 years, as shown in Figures 2 and 3, based on data from the National Bureau of Statistics of China.

A study conducted by the University of Texas and the Gerson Lehrman Group (*The Hanification of Xinjiang, China: The Economic Effects of the Great Leap West*, by Amy Liu and Kevin Peters, 2017) studied the question of Han migrants into Xinjiang gaining more benefit from the massive development of the region than the indigenous Uyghur people. The government launched the "Great Leap West" in 1999 to develop the interior of the country. There has always been a large Han minority in Xinjiang, but that minority has now grown to be nearly equal the Uyghur population in numbers. The total population of 22 mil-

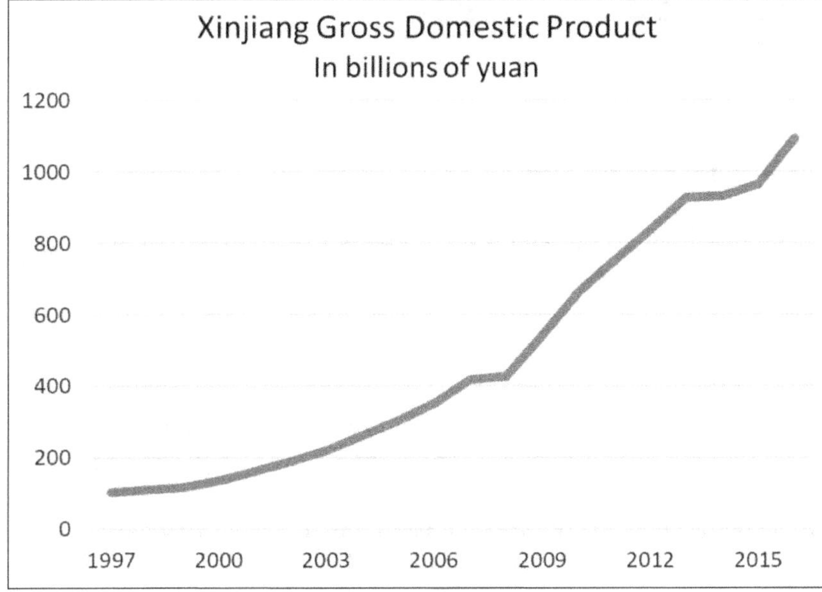

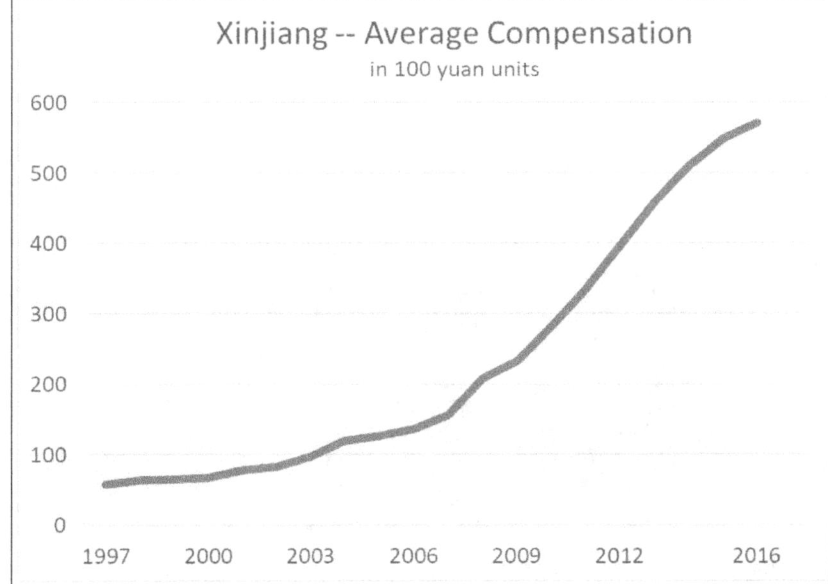

additional $22 billion in developing new oil and natural gas resources in Xinjiang, as part of the move to reduce the country's dependence on coal.

After detailed studies of wages and standards of living, this University of Texas study concluded: "While the Han migrants have benefitted immensely from the development programs, the Uyghurs have enjoyed the benefits as well." Over the past two years, the central government has directed increasing amounts of credit into the southern region of Xinjiang, south of the Taklamakan Desert, the second largest sand desert in the world. Two paved highways now cross the Taklamakan, 562 km and 436 km long. The southern region is poorer, and also has a higher concentration of Uyghurs. The investments are focused on agriculture, especially water and irrigation, where cotton and fruits are grown.

The southern region has 1.6 million people living below the poverty line, part of the approximately 30 million Chinese still living in poverty. Having lifted 700 million Chinese out of poverty over the past decades, China has made the commitment to ending poverty altogether by 2020. Already in Xinjiang, besides providing jobs with a living wage to millions of Uyghurs, *People's Daily* reported that 461,000 rural residents have been relocated from destitute regions to new towns in 2018 alone, where they have been provided with housing and jobs.

The miracle performed by China since the 1978 beginning of the reform and opening up under Deng Xiaoping, and escalating under Xi Jinping's Belt and Road Initiative, is a boon for all mankind, based on the win-win concept that joint development is a common aim of all nations and all people. It is to be hoped that the meetings now scheduled between President Trump and President Xi Jinping following the midterm elections in the United States, will resolve conflicting issues between the two great nations within the higher principle of cooperation and co-development of the world and beyond.

lion—with thirteen major ethnic groups—includes 8.8 million Uyghurs, 7.7 million Han, and 1.4 million Kazaks.

The study reports that the massive infrastructure development in Xinjiang includes the building and expansion of airports, highway, roads, railroads, telecommunications networks, high-voltage electrical transmission lines, and more. There was $85 billion in new investments in Xinjiang in 2017, excluding oil investments, which were billions more. In July, China National Petroleum Corporation announced that it would invest an

II. Science and Scientific Method

The Parker Solar Probe: Rendezvous with Our Exuberant Sun

by Janet G. West

> *"Ad astra per aspera."*
> It is a rough road which leads to the stars.

Oct. 12—If you've seen a picture of a total eclipse of the Sun, or a video clip, or had the great, and truly awe-inspiring privilege of experiencing one—at the point of totality, the corona becomes visible, bursting out from behind the disk of the Moon. It is to this corona region that the Parker Solar Probe, launched on August 12, 2018, has been deployed; it is scheduled to arrive around November 1.

As of this writing, the Probe has successfully transmitted "first-light data" from each of its four instruments, demonstrating that they're working well (the data serves for calibration by using celestial landmarks), and has had its first flyby past Venus on October 3.

Humanity has waited many centuries for this kind of mission; waiting for technology, design and materials to catch up with the dream of "touching the Sun."[1]

Who is Dr. Eugene Parker?

The solar wind (as we understand it) is shot out from the Sun's corona at speeds approaching one million mph and can represent about one million tons of matter being emitted per second, in all directions. We experience it (most commonly) in the spectacular effects of its interaction with Earth's magnetic fields and atmosphere in the Aurorae (the Northern Lights and Southern Lights).[2]

It was Johannes Kepler (1571-1630), the Father of Modern Astronomy, who first hypothesized that there was some sort of "wind" or "pressure" emanating from the Sun, which caused the tails of comets always to point away from the Sun in their orbits.

But sunlight "pressure" itself couldn't account for all of the behavior of comets and their tails; a fuller ex-

FIGURE 1

NASA

Eugene N. Parker as a young man.

planation would wait until 1943, when Cuno Hoffmeister (1892-1968), a German scientist, hypothesized the existence of a "solar wind." Later, in 1947, Ludwig Biermann (1907-1986) also independently pointed to the existence of "solar corpuscular radiation."

Dr. Eugene N. Parker hypothesized in 1957 how the solar wind functions,[3] and developed concepts to de-

---

1. The concept for a "Solar Probe" dates back to "Simpson's Committee" of the Space Science Board (National Academy of Sciences, 24 October 1958).

2. "Unlocking the Secrets of the Aurorae," *EIR*, Vol. 45, No. 17, April 27, 2018.

3. Dr. Parker coined the term, "solar wind."

scribe the cascade of energy from the Sun in a complex and dynamic system of plasmas, magnetic fields and high-energy particles. His theory has also suggested the existence of small and persistent "nanoflares" on the surface of the Sun which could help explain the super-heated corona. He has explained that in his observations of the behavior of comets and the Sun, he immediately saw the interactions as hydrodynamic (in a spherical geometry). He worked out four lines of "simple" algebraic formulae to describe it and wrote up his findings in his first paper in 1958, "Dynamics of the Interplanetary Gas and Magnetic Fields." He was 30 years old. [**Figure 1**]

Among his assertions was that the solar wind *had to be supersonic*, and this led to the development of the Sweet-Parker theory of magnetic reconnection to account for it.[4]

When he submitted his paper to the *Astrophysical Journal* (whose editor was astrophysicist Subrahmanyan Chandrasekhar), one of the reviewers commented, "This is ridiculous! Before you write a scientific paper, you should at least take the trouble of going to the library and reading up on the subject!" Dr. Parker's response to Chandrasekhar was, "Well, he couldn't find anything wrong with it—it must be pretty good!" Chandrasekhar overrode the reviewer's objections and put the paper through for publication.[5]

Still, Dr. Parker's ideas were considered very controversial at the time. Some claimed that it would be impossible for anything supersonic to be generated from the Sun, while others insisted that there was nothing but Newton's "empty space" between the planets and the Sun. "It was something most people couldn't seem to swallow. They expressed stern disbelief," Parker said in an interview earlier this year.

But, it was the physics of hydrodynamics that convinced Parker that the solar wind *had to exist*, not empirical evidence per se (although that became available as space exploration expanded).[6] Most of his peers

Dr. Parker watches the launch of the Solar Probe.

didn't believe him, but that didn't deter him, and with the help of some allies in the scientific community, he forged ahead.[7] He went against the "popular opinion" of his time.

Recently, not only did NASA rename the Probe after him (the first spacecraft ever named after a living scientist), but also awarded him the Distinguished Public Service Medal—the highest honor by NASA for an individual who isn't a government employee, recognizing excellence in scientific work for NASA and the nation.

Dr. Parker has made clear that he's deeply honored, and that he's very happy that he's been proven right, but at the same time he congratulates the engineers, technicians and scientists who made it possible: "They're the *real* heroes!" He has also said that he considers the Probe itself to be "heroic" and a "brave spacecraft" to get so close to the Sun. [**Figure 2**]

One of Dr. Parker's collaborators, Dr. Angela Olinto, the University of Chicago's Dean of Physical Sciences, commented "This represents science at its best—when you can create a theory about something, and then go out with an experiment and prove that it's right.... Most of the time, we don't get it right."

Dr. Parker has emphasized the reality that just because you're right, that doesn't mean you can expect to have an easy path; he acknowledges that most science is made by someone's standing up and proposing something very, very controversial.

If you look to the leading scientific minds of the

---

4. Magnetic reconnection refers to the breaking and reconnecting of oppositely directed magnetic fields lines in a plasma. In the process, magnetic field energy is converted to plasma kinetic and thermal energy. Observed in solar flares, controlled thermonuclear fusion devices (especially tokamaks) and magnetospheres of planets. In hydrodynamics a similar effect is called "reconnection of vorticity" or "reconnection of quantized vortex elements."

5. See https://youtu.be/WH_TC9VzMUA

6. Once Mariner II got outside of the bow shock of Earth's magnetosphere, it was able to observe solar activity and magnetic field around the Sun and confirmed the existence of the solar wind.

7. Parker jokes about the irony that he's still here—sixty years later—and the people who disagreed with him are not.

past—going back to Plato—from Kepler to Einstein, from Madame Curie to Rosalind Franklin, from Leibniz to LaRouche—those who have made fundamental breakthroughs in scientific thought have always had to oppose the prevailing "popular opinion"—which can sometimes appear to be as strong as solar wind, but usually just winds up as a lot of hot air.

In the current culture that dominates most of North America and Europe, in which the wacky pagan-environmentalist paradigm prevails, it can take some courage to stand up for what one *knows* to be true (in the Platonic sense of knowing)—but the future of humanity depends upon it. One of our biggest challenges isn't the environmentalists themselves, but that many among us would prefer to be fooled, to be humored into meaningless and wasteful activity such as "recycling," and to believe that the world is "overpopulated"—because by not thinking for yourself, you manage to shirk your responsibility for the future of mankind. Humanity needs courageous people to step forward now and help lead America (and other nations) into a New Paradigm. We can learn a lesson by deliberating on the writings of the great German poet, Friedrich Schiller:

> Dare to be wise! A spirited courage is required to triumph over the impediments that the indolence of nature as well as the cowardice of the heart oppose to our instruction. It was not without reason that the ancient myth made Minerva issue fully armed from the head of Jupiter, for it is with warfare that this instruction commences. From its very outset it has to sustain a hard fight against the senses, which do not like to be roused from their easy slumber. The greater part of men are much too exhausted and enervated by their struggle with want, to be able to engage in a new and severe contest with error. Satisfied if they themselves can escape from the hard labor of thought, they willingly abandon to others the guardianship of their thoughts. And if it happens that nobler necessities agitate their soul, still they cling with a greedy faith to the formula that the state and the church hold in reserve for such cases. If these unhappy men deserve our compassion, those others deserve our just contempt, who, though set free from those necessities by more fortunate circumstances, yet willingly bend to their yoke. These latter persons prefer this twilight of obscure ideas, where the feelings have more intensity, and the imagination can at will create convenient chimeras, to the rays of truth which put to flight the pleasant illusions of their dreams. They have founded the whole structure of their happiness on these very illusions, which ought to be combatted and dissipated by the light of knowledge, and they would think they were paying too dearly for a truth which begins by robbing them of all that has value in their sight. It would be necessary that they should be already sages to love wisdom: a truth that was felt at once by him to whom philosophy owes its name.
>
> It is therefore not going far enough to say that the light of understanding only deserves respect when it reacts on the character; to a certain extent it is from the character that this light proceeds; for the road that terminates in the head must pass through the heart. Accordingly, the most pressing need of the present time is to educate the sensibility, because it is the means, not only to render efficacious in practice the improvement of ideas, but to call this improvement into existence.[8]

The Measure of Man

Mankind developed navigation by using his mind and powers of observation, using the Sun by day and the stars by night. He used the rising and setting of the Sun and the yearly cycles to *orient* cities and major monuments. Humanity expanded the science of astronavigation in very ancient times; there is evidence of sea-faring peoples successfully sailing from the regions of Polynesia to the coasts of South America; much later, the Vikings were renowned for their ability to navigate on cloudy days by using the unique properties of the Iceland Spar (or Sun Stone).

Astronavigation uses angular measurements ("sights") between a celestial body (Sun, Moon) and the visible horizon, to locate one's position on Earth. There are several methods of doing this, which the reader may explore on your own.

A unique feature of Earth lies between the Tropic of Cancer and the Tropic of Capricorn, over which the Sun's rays reach the surface at a point which is perpendicular to it. This is called the "subsolar point" (or Lahaina noon, in Hawaii), which may not occur exactly at

---

8. Letter III of *Letters on the Aesthetic Education of Man*, by Friedrich Schiller. Translator unknown. S.E. Cassino and Company, 1884.

plus.google.com

At the Subsolar Point, there are no shadows for vertical objects.

noon, but in which an object eerily casts no shadow. [**Figure 3**]

The approximate measurement of the circumference of the Earth was first executed by Eratosthenes of Cyrene (276 BC - 194 BC), using this astronomical event. His method was to use an observation first in Syene (now Aswan, Egypt), known to be a certain distance from Alexandria, Egypt. On the summer solstice at noon, a vertical measure in a sundial cast no shadow in Syene but cast a shadow of about 7.2 degrees from the vertical in Alexandria at the same time and date. Knowing the distance of the two cities, and assuming that due to the great size and distance of the Sun, that its rays to the two points were practically parallel, he calculated that the circumference of the Earth was about 250,000 stadia, or roughly 24,500 miles—very close to current measurements, which show it to be in the range of 24,860 to 24,901 miles.

With some thought and effort, this could be replicated in schools in different cities of a known distance apart, such that the students would then actually come to know the Earth's approximate circumference. So, why isn't this being done?[9]

In a similar way, anyone in the Northern Hemisphere can notice that the days after the Autumnal Equinox become shorter, and in December we'll experience the Winter Solstice, the shortest day of the year.

Using either a camera, or daily sightings on a fixed object (such as a window), if you note the position of the Sun in the sky at the same time of day throughout the year, the Sun traces out a figure-eight (analemma) in the sky above, like a string of pearls flung across the firmament. In one's mind's eye, imagine: What would the relationship of the Earth be to the Sun in order to account for this? What is the tilt of the Earth, in relation to the plane of its orbit around the Sun? What causes the change of the seasons? [**Figure 4**] and [**Figure 5**]

---

9. LaRouchePAC Live, "How the Empire Gets You Not to Think ..."

FIGURE 4

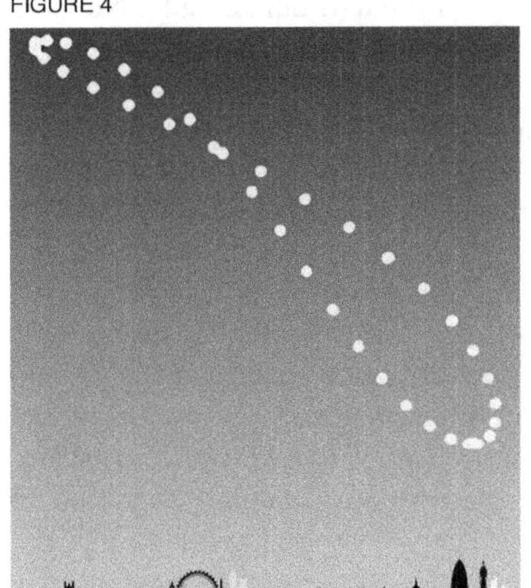

The annual path of the Sun—the analemma.

FIGURE 5

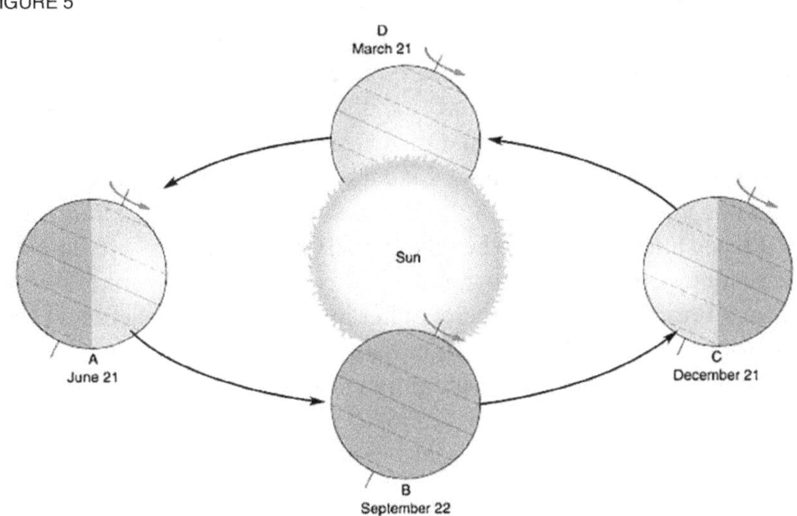

The annual solstices and equinoxes.

Painting by Edwin Henry Landseer, 1851

"Scene from A Midsummer Night's Dream, Titania and Bottom," (Bottom as a Donkey).

Looking at Figure 4, the upper point on the left is the Summer Solstice, the lower right is the Winter Solstice, and the midpoint represents the equinoxes. On a globe, the northern-most point is represented by the Tropic of Cancer and the southern is the Tropic of Capricorn, where the Sun is directly overhead.

Since all of this is observable to the average person, who is it that wants to prevent you from using your mind?

'Be Afraid... Be Very Afraid...'

They walk among us ... like the "living dead".... They look human, but they are something quite different. Like the ominous "pod-people" of the 1978 *Invasion of the Body Snatchers*, these counterfeit humanoids can usually be detected by their leech-like attachment to the viewpoint that man is simply a beast and is on a par with the animals. Like the infection of a trematode in a garden snail, the "standards" imposed by the science mafia in order to be recognized (and receive grant money), insidiously poison the budding scientific thinker or researcher, turning him or her into something akin to the zombie-like, parasite-filled snail, slowly proceeding up a stem, doing the puppet-master's bidding—to be consumed by a predator. Those who resist are punished—their funding is cut, or they are ostracized and banished.

These "standards" are then propagated like spores, through the media, through foundations and academia, and throughout every level of education down to kindergarten, to further corrupt the general population.

Look at a list of the so-called "most influential scientists" today,[10] and what do you find?

For example, examine the likes of James Watson, Jane Goodall, and the late Stephen Hawking. Who are these "experts"? Are we to behave like that fabled Queen of the Fairies, Titania, in Shakespeare's play *Midsummer Night's Dream*, that we can be induced to admire and fall in love with asses? [**Figure 6**]

Stephen Hawking has been best known for his book, *A Brief History of Time*; Lyndon H. LaRouche demolishes its premises in an article in *EIR*:

Now, to the chapter in question ["The Arrow of Time"]. In the second paragraph of the chapter, Hawking writes: "Up to the beginning of this century people believed in an absolute time. That is, each event could be labelled by a number called 'time' in a unique way, and all good clocks would agree on the time interval between two events...." That statement of his, is false.[11]

LaRouche then discusses the historical division in science—on one side, the real pioneers such as Karl Gauss, Bernhard Riemann, and Gottfried Leibniz (among others); and on the anti-human side, Newton, James Clerk Maxwell and Bertrand Russell. He decorticates Hawking's "respectable" veneer by exposing the false axioms underlying Hawking's outlook.

James Watson? Do you really believe he was a "co-discoverer" of the double-helix structure of DNA? This demonstrates how thoroughly various agencies and media cooperate to "airbrush out" anyone they don't like. The true discoverer was Rosalind Franklin, who created the first X-ray diffraction images of DNA and the interpretation of those images.

And, Jane Goodall? *The "Chimp Lady"?!* A "scientist" who has the insolence to compare mankind to

---

10. See, for example, the list on www.bigthink.com
11. "Mathematicians Who Can't Tell Time," *EIR* Vol. 24, No. 23, May 30, 1997.

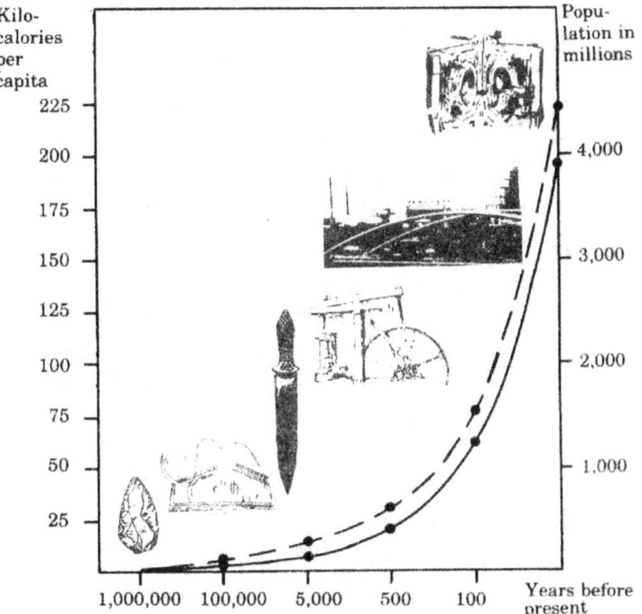

LaRouche, *There Are No Limits to Growth*

Historical increases in energy flux-density.

apes? According to a recent documentary,

> Goodall also admits that her looks, which gar-
> nered a lot of attention, helped her get publicity
> while trying to secure funding for her research
> projects. As she notes, "And it didn't harm either
> that I wasn't born ugly. I think it helped."[12]

So, don't let these "experts" make a monkey out of
you!

Every Human Being a Scientist!

"But," you argue, "shouldn't science be left to the
'experts'? And, if a majority of 'experts' agree on something, then it *must* be true, right? After all, *who am I* to
refute them?"

In reality, mankind's progress over the millennia is
due to our unique creative capabilities, which set mankind superior to and separate from the beasts. One
might say that to be human is to think scientifically, or
with the gift of Reason.

Going back to at least the time of the Babylonian
Empire (about 1792 B.C.), there have been oligarchies

and priesthoods that kept certain types of knowledge
secreted away, to rule over men as beasts, and to keep
them in darkness. But there has been a different tradition which has implicitly (or explicitly) recognized and
encouraged the quality in man which enables and requires creative discovery, upwards in history through
the Renaissance, and to the founding of the truly revolutionary United States of America. That quality has led
not only to an increase in population, but an increase in
potential relative population-density, through technological progress. [**Figure 7**]

As economist and statesman LaRouche wrote in his
1983 book, *There Are No Limits to Growth*:

> The simplest of the physical principles involved
> in choosing among energy sources is that the
> higher the level of energy-flux density, the more
> efficient the energy source is. Not only is less
> heat wasted, but the higher the energy-flux den-
> sity, the greater the potential of the process-heat
> to accomplish work.
>
> To appreciate the importance of this … we
> must consider another important kind of figure.
> This figure … is named potential relative popu-
> lation density.…
>
> Given a population inhabiting a certain terri-
> tory, and let that territory be measured in square-
> kilometers of habitable area. By developing and
> using the natural resources available in that area,
> how many people can be maintained through the
> work of the population's labor force? On the av-
> erage, the answer is given as the average number
> of persons per average square-kilometer. Per-
> sons per square-kilometer is population-density.
>
> That figure is not an adequate measurement.
> Land varies in quality, so that one square-kilo-
> meter is not of the same quality for human habi-
> tation as another square-kilometer. Those desir-
> able qualities of land, which express such
> differences, are variable qualities. Man may im-
> prove the land or deplete it.
>
> The quality of land is the net result of com-
> bined depletions and improvements of its quali-
> ties. Therefore, we say that the value of all square
> kilometers are not the same; they are different, and
> they are variable. Therefore, we must measure
> population-density in terms of relative qualities of
> the land inhabited: relative population-density.

---

12. See https://www.yahoo.com/lifestyle/jane-goodall-looks-helped-
career-didnt-harm-either-wasnt-born-ugly-120040793.html

The present level of population is not necessarily a measurement of what the population level could be. We must determine what that population could become, as a maximum, given the kinds of production technologies presently in use. What is the potential level of population, given those technologies? That is the general meaning of potential relative population-density.

We have already indicated that the potential relative population-density of primitive society is about 0.06 to 0.10/square kilometer: about 10 millions maximum population. There exist today approximately 4.5 billions individuals,[13] more than 100 times the levels of primitive man. Since a factor of "10" is called one order of magnitude, this means that mankind has raised its potential relative population-density by two orders of magnitude. With full use of existing levels of technology, combined with the thermonuclear, directed-beam, and bio-technology coming into existence now, our planet could sustain a population of tens of billions of persons, and at an average standard of living higher than that for the United States during the early 1970s: a rise above primitive society by three order of magnitude.

No beast, or any other lower form of life could willfully increase in potential relative population-density by even one order of magnitude. [Emphasis added] Man is fundamentally different from the beasts. Man is not merely a creature of instinctive potentialities, a mere creature of animal-like perceptions of pleasure and pain. Man is somehow very different. Man has the potential of Reason, the power to make creative discoveries which advance his scientific knowledge, and to convert such scientific advances into advances in technology. We are able to uncover, with increasing perfection, the lawful, universal principles which order universal creation, and to master nature with increasing power, through guiding ourselves to change our ways of behavior in accordance with universal laws.

The successive technological advances accumulated by human culture … have increased man's potential relative population density by between two and three orders of magnitude.

This technological progress, this increase in human potential, has been accomplished by an increasing command over energy. Beginning with the agricultural revolution, and ocean fishing in boats earlier, mankind has increased the amount of useful energy available to the average individual, and has increased the number of kilowatt-hours' value of the amount of usable energy obtained by society per square-kilometer. Today, we can roughly measure the fertility of agricultural land by the amount of "artificial energy" used per hectare by the farmer: chemical energy of fertilizers, trace element additions, pesticides, and electrical and other industrially produced energy forms used for irrigation, powered machinery, and so forth. Similarly, in industry and transportation, the productive powers of the average member of the labor force are measured in first approximation by the amount of industrially-produced energy used per capita.

This technological progress is not merely an available option. The authors of the *Limits to Growth* are right on one point, although perhaps this was an unintentional feature of their book. *If, at any point, we halt technological progress, the society foolish enough to do such a thing condemns itself to die.* [Emphasis added]

There is no such thing as the "balance of nature"; the idea of a "homeostatic" universe is a fraud. Anyone who promotes "zero-growth" for mankind is proposing a genocide that would dwarf that of the Nazis. The world needs more people, living at a higher living standard than the most advanced areas of the world currently enjoy. This can be done through technological progress, and the development of new resources and energy sources with a high energy-flux density, such as controlled thermonuclear fusion.

It is especially through space exploration that we can advance our civilization, and better understand nonlinear events and man's true purpose and mission in the universe.

The Spacecraft with Attitude

The Parker mission is part of NASA's "Living with a Star" program, and our Sun is the only star to which we can get very close, allowing observations of the corona—and the solar wind, which accelerates rapidly

---

13. We are now edging close to 8 billion people on Earth.

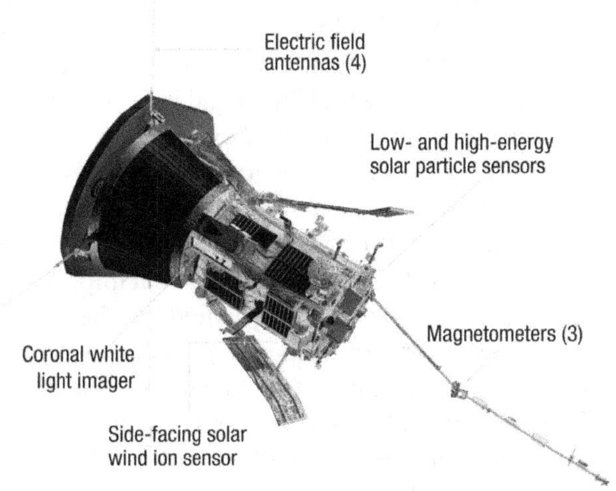

The Parker Solar Probe.

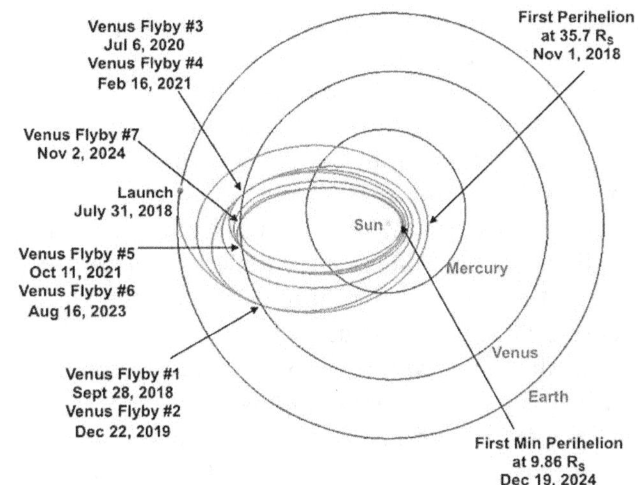

Successive orbits of the Probe.

from subsonic to supersonic—and a better understanding of the complex dynamics that affect space weather. The mission to send a probe to the Sun has been in development for about ten years, and has involved hundreds (if not thousands) of engineers, technicians, and other scientists to bring it to the launch pad. [**Figure 8**]

The Probe will be traveling at 430,000 mph in its journey around the Sun. By comparison, the Earth is moving at about 67,000 mph in our orbit around the Sun (and the entire galaxy is moving at about 1.3 million mph through space).

The original plan was to have the Parker Solar Probe orbit over the poles of the Sun, and to use Jupiter for gravity assist, but this would have meant only two solar passes. However, the then project manager for the mission, Andy Dantzler (who passed away in 2011 at age 49), intervened, and suggested that instead the mission move to an orbit on the ecliptic, which allows more robust readings of the solar wind. This new trajectory allows *over 900 hours* within about 8 million miles of the Sun! This underscores the key role that an individual leader can have, at the right moment.

The mission has three primary science objectives, to—

• Trace the flow of energy that heats and accelerates the solar corona and solar wind;

• Determine the structure and dynamics of the plasma and magnetic fields at the sources of the solar wind; and

• Explore mechanisms that accelerate and transport energetic particles.

It is more difficult to launch toward the Sun than to launch into the outer Solar system. This has to do with orbital mechanics—the study of how natural forces influence the motions of planets and comets, as well as of rockets, satellites and other space-bound technology.[14] It might seem "effortless" to fall toward the Sun—since its gravity is so pervasive—but the Earth is also moving at great speed, and, along with the stability of the orbit itself, it resists the pull from the Sun. To travel from the Earth to Mars only requires a slight increase in orbital speed; but to go inwards to the inner Solar system, the momentum must be slowed down.

Normally, when a "gravity-assist" is used by a spacecraft, it moves on a trajectory into a narrow gravitational band around a planet, to sling the spacecraft out further at a faster rate of speed. But, when moving inwards within the Solar system, the gravity-assist is used to slow down a spacecraft. The Probe will make 24 passes around Venus during its lifetime; on its final passes, it will fly closer than 4 million miles from the Sun. After its mission, the Probe will drop further into the corona, and merge with the Sun. [**Figure 9**]

The big design issue for the Probe was how to design the instruments such that they can not only withstand

---

14. Unbenownst to many, a certain IPCC expert, in a brief moment of sanity, was planning a manned space mission to the Sun; but he decided on a night launch to prevent the spacecraft from burning up.

heat and radiation enough to make significant measurements, but also withstand the coldness of space as it swings out around Venus.

Since some of the instruments measure magnetic fields, the engineers had to ensure as little magnetic interference as possible by the guidance and power systems. As the Probe passes by the Sun, it will be taking measurements, and then as it orbits back around Venus, it will talk to Earth about three times a week to download its data and transmit a beacon tone which indicates spacecraft health and status.

The instruments on the Probe and short descriptions of what they measure are as follows:

FIELDS—This instrument suite of five antennas will measure the scale and shape of the electric and magnetic fields of the Sun's near atmosphere, including the waves and turbulence within the heliosphere, to better understand its activity, especially magnetic field reconnection, in which magnetic field lines break and then realign explosively.

Four of the antennas will project beyond the heat shield, experiencing temperatures in the range of 2,500°F. The fifth will remain behind the heat shield, and is set perpendicular to the others, so that altogether they can recreate a three-dimensional picture of the solar wind.

WISPR—The Wide-Field Imager for the Parker Solar Probe is the only imaging instrument onboard, taking images of the coronal mass ejections (CMEs). It will look at the large-scale structure of the corona and solar wind before the spacecraft flies through it. The device will be behind the heat shield, and uses specially designed baffles and occulters to reflect and absorb stray light that may be reflected by other parts of the Probe. The WISPR uses two cameras with radiation-hardened Active Pixel Sensor CMOS detectors.

SWEAP—This is the Solar Wind Electrons, Alphas and Protons investigation, and uses two complementary instruments: The Solar Probe Cup (SPC, aka Faraday Cup), and the Solar Probe Analyzers, or SPAN. These instruments will count the particles within the solar wind (such as electrons, protons and helium ions) and measure properties such as velocity, polarization, density and temperature of the solar wind and coronal plasma. This instrument, along with the others, will be able to image the Sun in three dimensions.

IS☉IS—Incorporating the symbol for the Sun in its acronym (pronounced "EE-sis"), the Integrated Science Investigation of the Sun uses two complementary instruments to measure particles across a wide range of energies, and will help the investigation of their lifecycles—how they are generated, where they come from, how they become accelerated and how they continue to travel throughout interplanetary space.

However, the real "star of the show" is the design and construction of the systems that protect and power the craft. The Probe has an autonomous computer system onboard that can gauge the heat impacting it, and can move the solar panels behind the heat shield, or bring them forward, depending on the surroundings. When it goes behind the Sun, it can't receive or transmit data or commands from Earth, so it is also able to detect its orientation, such that if the bulk of the craft isn't safely behind the heat shield, it will precisely maneuver itself to point the heat shield directly at the Sun, to safeguard the instruments (the center of gravity must be behind the center of force on the shield).

The solar panels have shoulder joints, and so can fold like wings behind the heat shield. They and the entire craft are enveloped in a cooling system, because—ironically—the Sun's heat and power are too great for solar panels to withstand once it gets close. At its closest point, the panels will fold up almost entirely, with only the tips peeking out from behind the shield—and this will provide more than sufficient power for the craft and all of its instruments.

TPS—The Thermal Protection System comprises the heat shield and the cooling system. The heat shield is eight feet in diameter, weighs about 160 pounds, is about 97% air, and must safeguard the entire craft in its shadow. There are two panels of superheated carbon-carbon, sandwiching a lightweight 4.5-inch-thick carbon foam core. The Sun-facing side is also sprayed with a specially formulated white ceramic coating to help reflect as much as the Sun's heat as possible. This means that although the Sun-facing side will be around 2,500°F, the shaded side will be in the range of 80-85°F.

But, the instruments will only tell part of the story; the issue is: what is the mindset of those interpreting the data?

Heavenly Magnetism

Using your Reason, take an astronomical step back from Earth, as if we were viewing it from many millions of miles out in space; we see that our globe, as well as much of the Solar system, lives *within* the atmo-

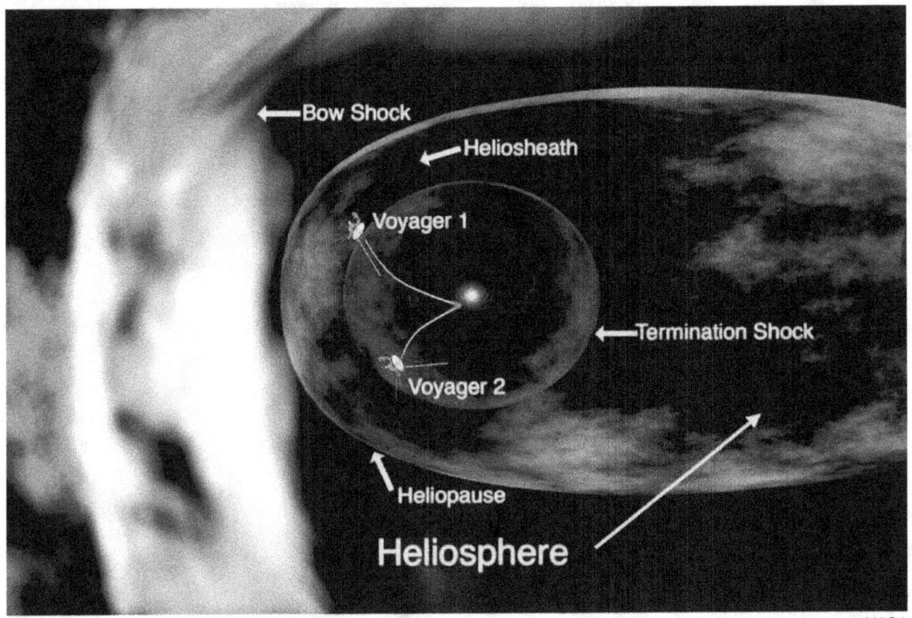

Artist's representation showing our Solar system as a blue sphere with the yellow Sun in its center, surrounded by the lighter blue, oval-shaped Heliosheath, within interstellar space.

sphere of the Sun. There are complicated relationships between the orbits, the solar wind and the magnetospheres of the planets, which are still under investigation.

Figure 10 shows the immense environment within which the Earth is bathed. The solar wind extends far out beyond the Solar system; beyond it is interstellar space. Earth and all the planets of our Solar system are in constant interaction with the solar wind, as well as cosmic rays from various origins.

Dr. Parker hypothesized the nature of the magnetic field generated by the Sun, and the shape that it takes as the Sun rotates (also known as the "heliospheric current sheet"). **Figure 11A** and **11B** show first the static picture of the electromagnetic sheet (not so smooth in reality), and the dynamic view demonstrating how the field changes with the 11-year minimum-maximum activity cycle of the Sun (view the 15-second animation of Figure 11B). This has been generally associated with increasing and decreasing activity of sunspots, but the details of that interaction are currently unknown.

The Sun's magnetic field is reversing in polarity when this occurs; the waves increase in size during this reversal every 11 years. Within these cycles, the shape and intensity of the Sun's magnetic fields, sunspots and solar wind are also changing, which in turn affect the intensity of thunderstorms and the frequency of lightning bolts here on Earth, as well as other space weather.[15]

---

15. "Sun's magnetic field affects frequency of lightning strikes on Earth," https://physicsworld.com/a/suns-magnetic-field-affects-frequency-of-lightning-strikes-on-earth/

NASA

Static representation of the heliospheric current sheet with inner planets.

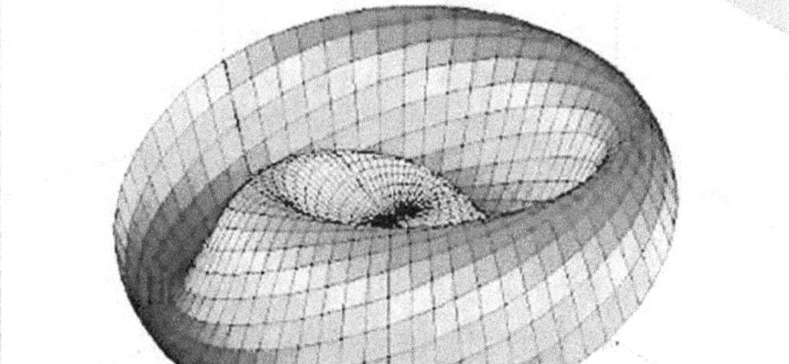

Benacor on YouTube

Screenshot from a computer animation of the heliospheric current sheet during the Sun's 11-year magnetic cycle.

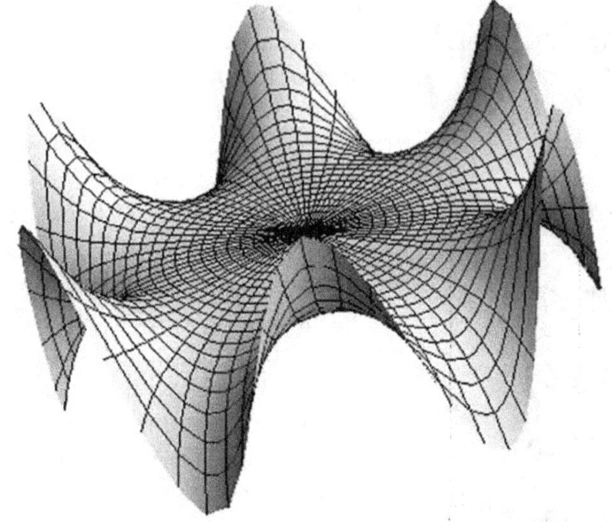

Representation of a constant negative Gauss curvature.

It is currently unknown exactly how these variations occur; currently, there's no known correlation between the flipping of the Sun's magnetic poles and the Earth's. Ironically, although cosmic rays are an ever-present challenge to space travel, the sheath has a dampening effect on them, such that the inner Solar system is somewhat shielded; ongoing research is investigating this activity to answer these questions.

Figure 11B reminds one of the topography of a Gaussian Surface [**Figure 12**], especially if one imagines such a surface in rotation. What relationships could there be between these two representations, in terms of gravity and the electromagnetic fields?

And, it is important to bear in mind that our Solar system is also rotating within and around our entire galaxy, and so is subject to many influences. It is obvious that man's activities—such as "carbon emissions"—are minuscule compared to these massive dynamics. [**Figure 13**]

We have to get "up close and personal" with the Sun to begin to answer the many questions we have about the corona, solar flares and CMEs. As the Parker Solar Probe begins transmitting data, we anticipate breathtaking new discoveries and challenges.

Burning Questions

A schematic of the Sun's generalized structure can be found in any basic astronomy book

Size of the Earth compared to that of Sunspot 14886 on the white disk of the Sun.

or on many websites; an illustration is included here for quick reference. [**Figure 14**] And, even though illustrations and scientific articles refer to "the Sun's surface," it should be understood that no star truly

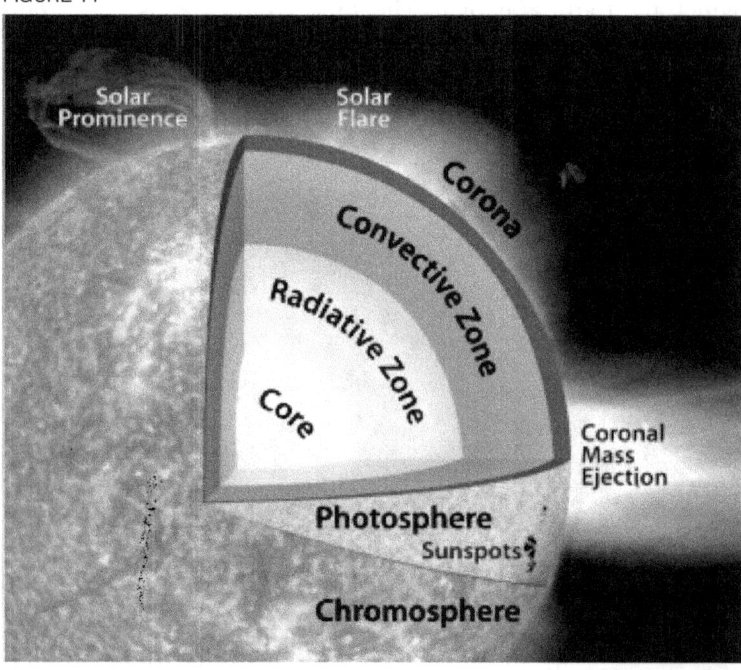

Representation of a cutaway of the Sun.

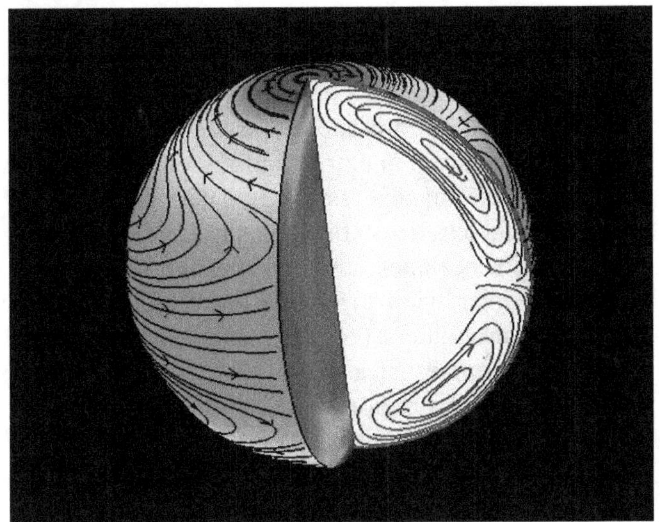

Utah Physics Department

Representation of a cutaway of the Sun, showing differential rotation in iso-rotation contours.

has a "surface," in our normal sense of the word.

The Sun accounts for 99.86% of the total mass of the Solar system. Its internal engine is fueled by nuclear fusion at its core; the Sun's magnetic field is generated by a hydromagnetic dynamo operating in its interior. It has been well-known that the Sun rotates differentially—the equatorial portion spins faster than the polar portion. [**Figure 15**] Additionally, the different layers within the Sun rotate at different speeds, and because of these motions a transition region is formed (a shearing effect), called the solar tachocline. This region lies between the radiative interior and the differentially rotating outer convective zone; it is believed to have a thickness of less than 0.05 solar radii, and is subjected to extreme radial and latitudinal shearing.

The mechanisms behind the formation of the tachocline are still disputed, but overall, scientific research attempting to forecast its behavior has had more success with a magnetohydrodynamic, over a merely hydrodynamic, representation. A particular quality of the tachocline is that it tenaciously defies the Second Law of Thermodynamics[16]—it remains stable

amidst turbulence both above and below it. Could something like this dynamic be replicated on Earth with an intent to assist the effort for controlled thermonuclear fusion?

Although still under intense research, the tachocline plays a key role in the process of magnetic field generation, not only in our Sun, but also in other stars. It seems to have the function of a dynamo in generating or amplifying magnetic fields, but it is beyond the scope of this article to discuss it in detail.

The Sun's convection zone generates sound waves continuously, due to this turbulence. The sound waves themselves will usually start at the surface and travel into the interior; due to the changing temperatures as they near the core, the sound waves bend, and are refracted back toward the surface. This continuous internal bombardment of the solar surface causes the entire Sun to vibrate, like a bell or a drum.[17] The sound waves form what is known as a "standing wave"; how might this relate to experiments done with a drum surface sprinkled with sand, in which different configurations develop spontaneously based on the frequency played? [**Figure 16**] Could this be fruitful line of work, possibly in relation to work on controlled fusion? Could a "standing wave" of plasma be generated to create a region of stability that could augment the fusion reaction? Could a plasma be "tuned?"

Recent research has shown that these sound waves are eventually conducted to the surface along magnetic field lines, which could help answer the question as to why the corona is so much hotter than the surface. Once at the surface, they propel fountains of hot gas (spicules) thousands of miles into space, overcoming a gravity pull which is about 27 times that of Earth's. They may also be a part of sunspot activity, although at this time the details are unknown.[18]

These sound waves are not transmitted into space, and are not heard, although NASA scientists have

---

16. The Second Law of Thermodynamics is a political fraud, explaining neither the development of the biosphere nor the mind of Man. For further discussion, see "Toppling the Tyranny of the 2nd Law of Thermodynamics," *EIR*, Vol. 39, No. 11, March 16, 2012.

17. See https://www.cora.nwra.com/~werne/eos/movies/oscillate.mpeg. This is a short and exaggerated animation of these sound waves. The regions of the Sun that are moving outward are red, and the blue are moving inward. If you were on the surface of the Sun, you would go up and down, like riding a wave. This only shows a single vibration mode; the Sun has many modes. Another short animation shows some actual motions of the Sun's surface: https://www.cora.nwra.com/~werne/eos/movies/hr_V_short.mpg

18. See https://www.space.com/3882-sound-waves-travel-sun-magnetic-field.html

"translated" some of the electromagnetic activity into audible sound.[19]

Coronal Mass Ejections

The corona is unstable and produces the solar wind, solar flares and coronal mass ejections (CMEs); millions of tons of highly magnetized plasma can erupt from the Sun, varying in speed from about 9,000 mph to over a million mph.[20]

As described on the website of the National Oceanographic and Atmospheric Agency (NOAA):

The more explosive CMEs generally begin when highly twisted magnetic field structures (flux ropes) contained in the Sun's lower corona become too stressed and realign into a less tense configuration—a process called magnetic reconnection. This can result in the sudden release of electromagnetic energy in the form of a solar flare; which typically accompanies the explosive acceleration of plasma away from the Sun—the CME. These types of CMEs usually take place from areas of the Sun with localized fields of strong and stressed magnetic flux; such as active regions associated with sunspot groups. CMEs can also occur from locations where relatively cool and denser plasma is trapped and suspended by magnetic flux extending up to the inner corona—filaments and prominences. When these flux ropes reconfigure, the denser filament or prominence can collapse back to the solar surface and be quietly reabsorbed, or a CME may result. CMEs travelling faster than the background solar wind speed can generate a shock wave. These shock waves can accelerate charged particles ahead of them—causing increased radiation storm potential or intensity.[21]

Although Earth is currently unprepared to withstand a powerful CME—which would blow out electrical transformers and severely disrupt satellite communications—one obvious solution would be to rebuild and upgrade our power grid and other technologies to make us less vulnerable. Power companies might opt to take transformers offline before a storm strikes, resulting in inconvenient blackouts, but not long-term devastation.

"Coronal holes" are another area of interest; they appear as dark areas in extreme ultraviolet (EUV) and soft X-ray solar images. They appear dark because they are cooler and less dense than the surrounding plasma, and are regions of open, unipolar magnetic fields. This allows the solar wind to escape more readily. When sighted by astronomers, they are monitored very closely by several agencies; if a major CME were to be expelled through this region, it could impact Earth massively. Larger, more expansive coronal holes can often be a source of high solar wind speeds that buffet Earth and its magnetosphere for several days.

Bringing Mysteries to Light

Adding to the mysteries of the Sun, recent research[22] has revealed that there is not one, but two types of solar wind (using the highly technical terms of "fast" and "slow"). The "slow" solar wind moves at around 700,000 mph, and it appears to be originating from the activity of the magnetic reconnections occurring constantly across the Sun. Understanding the source of the solar wind will also contribute to better forecasting of space weather. The fast solar wind can travel up to 1.7 million mph, and through study of its composition, scientists know that it emanates from the interior of "coronal holes"—areas in which the corona is darker and cooler.

The Goddard Space Flight Center team found something stunning about the slow wind:

"We found that the density and charge state composition of the slow solar wind rises and falls every 90 minutes, varying from what is normal [for] slow wind to what is [normal for] fast," Viall said. "But [its] speed was constant at a slow wind speed. This could only be created by magnetic reconnection at the Sun, tapping into both fast and slow wind source regions."[23]

19. See https://www.nasa.gov/feature/goddard/2018/sounds-of-the-sun
20. The largest solar storm on record on Sept. 1-2, 1859, known as the "Carrington Event," named for the British amateur astronomer Richard Carrington.
21. See www.swpc.noaa.gov
22. "Implications of L1 observations for slow solar wind formation by solar reconnection," https://agupubs.onlinelibrary.wiley.com/doi/full/10.1002/2016GL068607. The "L1" refers to a point in space between the Earth and Sun where the SOHO and Deep Space Climate Observatory are stationed. It gives an uninterrupted view of the Sun.
23. Nicholeen Viall, solar scientist with Goddard Space Flight Center; www.nasa.gov/feature/goddard/2016/swept-up-in-the-solar-wind

Another team member noted:

"It has been thought that the magnetosphere rang like a bell when the solar wind hit it with a sudden increase in pressure," said Larry Kepko, a magnetospheric scientist at Goddard. "We went in for a closer look and found these periodicities in the solar wind [itself]. The magnetosphere was acting more like a drum than a bell."[24]

"If we can understand this phenomenon here, where we can actually measure the magnetic field, we can get a better handle on how these fundamental physics processes take place in other places in the Universe," Viall said.

The physics of the corona and inner heliosphere connect the activity of the Sun to the environment and the technological infrastructure of Earth; discovering more will drive the physical understanding of the heliosphere, aurora, and magnetosphere of Earth and other planets; and it will help us to improve satellite communications, power grid issues, pipeline erosion, radiation exposure on airline flights, and astronaut safety.

What Lies Ahead

What the Probe will unveil about the nature of our Sun and our Universe in the coming seven years, can propel the economies of many nations of the world into increased productivity, and increase the optimism of young people to look forward to the future with excitement.

The larger mission is that we Americans must defeat the current British-led attack against President Donald Trump, so that he is free to carry out his election mandate; we must now bring all of humanity into the New Paradigm for Civilization, and address the fundamental economic questions which can provide a grand future. If we do not—and that rapidly—then the data transmissions from the Probe will fall upon deadened ears; our civilization will be incapable of responding.

As the economic genius Lyndon H. LaRouche reminds us:

Man is fundamentally different from the beasts.... Man has the potential of Reason, the power to make creative discoveries which advance his scientific knowledge, and to convert such scientific advances into advances in technology. We are able to discover, with increasing perfection, the lawful, universal principles which order universal creation, and to master nature with increasing power.[25]

It is notable that several of the engineers, technicians and scientists in leading positions in this mission are younger people in their twenties and thirties. What an optimistic perspective it would be to see this as the future of our youth, globally, instead of drug addiction, or worse—a job on Wall Street. One young astronomer summed it up beautifully: She remarked that some people look up at the stars and feel very small, but when she looks up at the heavens, she marvels that mankind is the only species able to contemplate and comprehend the Universe. The youth of America has a vital role to play in the creation of a new economic and cultural Renaissance, led in large part by the youthful thinkers within the LaRouche political movement worldwide.

China is already making great strides to help develop several African nations; think of the young adults in the many nations of Africa, and how they could be a part of a mission to develop our entire planet. If we don't address the question of economic and technological development, under present conditions they won't live long enough to participate in these opportunities.

Just as past generations have struggled and fought passionately—in a variety of ways—to ensure that we the living have the potential for a future, so we can also call up those strengths—and a quality of *agapē*— in ourselves and in others, to lay the foundations for those yet unborn to have a future worthy to be called human.

————

Editor's note: As we go to press, the Parker Solar Probe is due to make its first (and closest) of its 24 approaches to the Sun on November 5. It is already closer than any previous spacecraft.

————

25. *There are No Limits to Growth*, by Lyndon H. LaRouche. Club of Life, 1983.

————

24. Ibid.

A PASSAGE FROM "CLOAK & DAGGER, 101A"

"LaRouche's Personal Column" is occasionally written and published as the author may have a point he wishes to share with his friends through this special channel.

Executive Intelligence Review is printing this previously unpublished work by Lyndon H. LaRouche, Jr., which is referred to by Barbara Boyd in her article in this issue. We have retained all of the author's original punctuation and spelling. Square brackets are the author's.

by Lyndon LaRouche
March 7, 1984

The classroom education of a good "cloak and dagger" patriot might or might not, but should include a basic introductory course named "Cloak & Dagger, 101A." The instructor for this course is named Phil King. The following are a few of the remarks included in the first class-session of that course.

"The difference between a top-rate spy and the bungler is that the good spooks act on the basis of knowing that the most important things happening around them are the things that appear never to have happened at all. It is the things that aren't there that can really do you in, as the fellow said as he was falling down the empty elevator-shaft.

If you ever catch yourself drawing a conclusion from merely the list of facts you believe you have in your possession, stop yourself right there and think again. As the accountant told the judge, it was the crash that wasn't there that led to uncovering the embezzlement. Always be aware that you may have missed something of critical importance to making a decision. Make a list of the things which you didn't notice, things which might have happened, or which may not have happened, which you didn't notice.

"The most important events, among those you have overlooked, will usually be the non-events, events which never happened. The most important fact about a wedding is not the guest-list or the bride's costume, but the fact that the groom is missing.

"There are very few real-life situations in the work of a spook in which you will have the luxury of time available to spend hours re-thinking the situation in this way. You must learn the mental habits to perform these exercises quickly and automatically on your feet. You must tune these kinds of mental reflexes to the point that you think like this almost instantaneously. Most important of all, you must think like this whenever you're under the greatest immediate stress, at times the right or wrong decision made at that instant may decide whether you or your nation lives.

"Put it this way: you must reeducate your instincts. You must learn to stop reacting to stimuli. You must learn to react just as much to non-stimuli as to stimuli, to learn to react to both simultaneously. Obviously, you must retrain your instincts so that you reactions are the right ones. That's what this course is all about.

"What you must master is a method of thinking. You must work slowly at first, as we say in the military training programs, 'by the numbers.' You must apply this method of thinking to every kind of situation you experience, in the classroom here, or in the most ordinary and unimportant experiences in your daily personal life outside the classroom. You must make this method of thinking a habit, and you must use that habit in every aspect of even the most trivial kinds of decisions in daily personal life. You must learn never to think in any other way.

"Let's begin your training in this method by describing some basic rules. At first hearing, these basic rules may appear to be almost trivial, or may even appear to be only tricks with words. Don't be fooled; these rules are some of the most powerful rules of thinking that exist in this universe. Pay very close attention, and think carefully about these simple rules over and over again for the rest of your life; your life may depend upon it.

"RULE NUMBER ONE: The mere passage of time in which nothing is seen to happen, is the most important class of all events.

"RULE NUMBER TWO: Things by themselves have never happened in the history of the universe. A thing occurs only as an infinitesimal or larger transformation in the entire universe. Experience always occurs in a finite amount of time and a finite amount of displacement in space. Things as such do not exist; <u>only transformations in physical space-time exist</u>.

"RULE NUMBER THREE: Never make a decision based on the kinds of facts which can be completely identified by nouns, by statements of the syllogistic form, 'A is B.' A fact for you is never a fact, unless it is a statement of a <u>transitive verb</u>, a precise description of a transformation in the physical space-time observed: 'A happened in context B.'

"RULE NUMBER FOUR: You must add to the statement of the form 'A happened in context B,' 'If A happened in context B, then C should also have happened,' and also the statement 'If D also happened in context B, then either A did not happen, or the context of the happening is not B, but E.'

"RULE NUMBER FIVE: All judgments are echoes of underlying axiomatic assumptions concerning the laws of the universe as a whole, or of the special sub-phase of all physical space-time in which the matter of the judgment is properly immediately referenced. These assumptions are of two distinguishable but ultimately interdependent classes: the physical universe and the social universe. The critical evaluation of statements of the form, 'A happened in context B,' proceeds from examining the axiomatic assumptions implicit in that statement.

"I illustrate the thinking behind Rules Number Four and Five.

"Many among you have become acquainted with an hypothetical proposition of the following form. Assume that you are in some very exotic sort of space-vehicle. You awaken after a sleep, and discover that the stars around you don't look as they should. You ask yourself, 'Am I still in the same universe I was before I dropped off to sleep?' How would you go about answering that question?

"If you had been properly trained, as the study of the work of Karl Gauss and others after him implies, you would know exactly how to proceed. For those of you who are laymen in anything but elementary public-school geometry, I supply you the following illustration. Suppose you were a two-dimensional being moving in a two-dimensional universe, how would you discover whether that universe was either flat or curved in three-dimensional space? If you could discover that it was curved, how would you discover in what way the space was curved? You should know that the trigonom-etry of navigation in a flat-world is slightly different than the spherical trigonometry of a spherical surface, for example. In other words, there are certain principles of measurement of action which vary according to the kind of universe you are inside.

"For example, most people who have gone no further than elementary geometry believe that distances are measured by the pythagorean rule,

$$s = \sqrt{x^2 + y^2 + z^2} \; ,$$

or, with a bit more education, a corrected form of this expression. For purposes of initial discussion, we may say that as the pythagorean equation must be changed to measure action within physical space-time, we discover what kind of physical space-time we are experiencing, as from the inside.

"In crude approximation, we say that these required changes in the pythagorean tell us what kind of geometry we are living within. We say, therefore, in crude approximation, that we are living inside a geometry with a specific set of universal axioms.

"Apply this image of axiomatic geometry of physical space-time to the word 'context,' in the statement, 'A happened in the context of B.' If the portion of that statement, 'in the context of B' is valid, then if A happens, there are certain classes of events [happenings] which either must or could possibly occur within the same time-frame as A, and other classes of happenings which could not. In the case that D happened, as we identified this in Rule Number Four, then we are not observing 'context of B,' as we wrongly assumed, but are, instead, observing 'in the context of E.' Therefore we must apply Rule Number Five, to determine whether 'context E' is 'E_1, E_2, E_3, or ....'

"In other words we must always construct our judgments in the terms of the subjunctive mood of language, the mood of hypothesis.

"This applies to social universes just as it applies to physical universes.

"Individuals and groups of people are governed in their behavior by their acquired culture. Every culture is characterized by underlying assumptions concerning the nature of the universe, concerning the nature of the individuals within that universe, and concerning the range of the self-interests which individuals and groups have within that universe. These are of the form of the axioms of geometries of physical space-time. This is the key to applying the five rules we described to the social universe.

"We must combine the physical and social universes. People act according to the kind of geometry the axioms of their particular culture dictates—at least, most of the time. Their actions on the universe have consequences, in which these consequences are determined by the geometry of the physical space-time within which they are operating. The people judge the significance of those consequences according to their culture—most of the time. They will either react or not act to these consequences, as their culture required them to react—most of the time.

"We map an individual mind's psychology, or the collective psychology of people within a certain culture or sub-culture, by the same general method we employ to discover what kind of a physical universe we are within.

"By mastering this way of looking at experience, we are able to make valid statements of the form 'If A happened in context of B, then X_1, X_2, ... must also have happened, Y_1, Y_2, ... might possibly have happened, and Z_1, Z_2, ... could not possibly have happened.' 'If, on the contrary, Z_1 happened, then A happened in context E_1, rather than B, in which case X_{11}, X_{21}, ... must also have happened, Y_{11}, Y_{21}, ... might possibly have happened, and Z_{11}, Z_{21}, ... could not have happened.'

"The method we have just described is a very simplified description of a principle laid down by the great nineteenth century mathematical physicist, Bernhard Riemann. It is called the method of the 'unique experiment.' Extended to the practice of political-intelligence work, it is the essence of the method of a top-grade spook.

"For that reason, the next four weeks' classes will be devoted exclusively to mastery of the ABCs of what is called synthetic geometry. At first, you may think you are being sent back to learn what you should have begun to learn back in the Seventh Grade. 'Kid stuff,' will be the reaction of some among you. Block that understandable reaction. The problem is that you now accept, consciously or unconsciously, certain axioms of judgment and behaviors which are wrong. You must unlearn those wrong axioms, and master the right ones. That is the only way you will ever succeed in making the five rules your automatic response to each and every situation around you. Those five rules may save your life; they might help you to play an important part in saving our nation.

"Just make certain, when you walk through an elevator-doorway, that there is actually an elevator there."

30-30-30

FIDELIO

Journal of Poetry, Science, and Statecraft

From the first issue, dated Winter 1992, featuring Lyndon LaRouche on "The Science of Music: The Solution to Plato's Paradox of 'The One and the Many,'" to the final issue of Spring/Summer 2006, a "Symposium on Edgar Allan Poe and the Spirit of the American Revolution," *Fidelio* magazine gave voice to the Schiller Institute's intention to create a new Golden Renaissance.

The title of the magazine, is taken from Beethoven's great opera, which celebrates the struggle for political freedom over tyranny. *Fidelio* was founded at the time that LaRouche and several of his close associates were unjustly imprisoned, as was the opera's Florestan, whose character was based on the American Revolutionary hero, the French General, Marquis de Lafayette.

Each issue of *Fidelio*, throughout its 14-year lifespan, remained faithful to its initial commitment, and offered original writings by LaRouche and his associates, on matters of, what the poet Percy Byssche Shelley identified as, "profound and impassioned conceptions respecting man and nature."

Back issues are now available for purchase through the Schiller Institute website:

http://schillerinstitute.org/about/order_form.html

Update on the Coup: Desperate Measures To Stop Trump's Momentum!

The following are edited remarks from a presentation by Barbara Boyd to the October 27 Manhattan Project meeting in New York. A video of the full meeting is available.

We need a perspective, and we need to be laser-focused about where we've been and what happens right after the election. We have to take a step into the future. That's not to say that we're not facing an election which will, as we've said repeatedly, be historic and potentially determinative for this nation. There is not a lot to be said, however, about the outcome of the election itself, until it happens. That which can be said goes something as follows.

Should the Democrats take the House, they most certainly will move for the impeachment of Donald Trump, and Robert Mueller will most certainly slant his ultimate report to fuel it. The Democrats, who will then control the House Committees, will seek to investigate the President on every front in the hope of striking some form of gold which will move the public to accept his removal from

NextGen Climate Action
Thomas Steyer.

Bloomberg Philanthropies
Michael Bloomberg.

office. That much has already been bought and paid for by $250 million provided by Tom Steyer, Mike Bloomberg, and George Soros to flip the Congress.

For those who have been following our coverage of the coup closely, you know that Soros, Steyer, and Silicon Valley billionaires also funded British spy Christopher Steele to the tune of at least $50 million to keep up the British information warfare campaign against Donald Trump, after Christopher Steele was fired by the FBI. This effort is entirely aimed at removing Trump from office—as they would say it, by legal means or otherwise—as well as permanently destroying U.S.-Russian relations, and relations with China too. The billionaires are conducting this British intelligence operation on U.S. soil through the Penn Quarter Group, which is led by Dianne Feinstein's former chief Senate Intelligence staffer, Daniel Jones.

Impeachment will not work, if, as is probable, the Republicans not only hold the Senate, but expand their hold, based on Senators who have now staked their political fortunes to those

World Economic Forum
George Soros.

Xinhua

of the President. It is probably completely off the table if the Republicans hold the house or the Democratic majority is very, very, narrow.

The Rudiments of Political Intelligence

Those of you who have *not* been closely following what we have been saying, have been asking over and over again, "Why haven't the documents the President said would be declassified, been declassified? Why hasn't Rod Rosenstein been forced to appear before the Congress prior to the elections, to testify under oath about the *New York Times* story saying he wanted to wear a wire to gather evidence against Trump and remove him under the 25th Amendment?"

About eight months ago or so, I found a really, really profound Lyndon LaRouche personal column from 1984, titled "A Passage from Cloak and Dagger, 101A," and I forwarded it to some of my colleagues who were being somewhat reactive to the daily news cycle. They were thinking that they had to respond to what their contacts were bedeviling them with, based on the ritualized daily brainwashing which is performed by our corporate news media against this population. This is, of course, a complete fallacy in terms of what this organization's actual role is in history. We are not commentators on "reality" as proposed by a propaganda apparatus purposely designed to control and limit what human beings think. I will make sure the entire document by LaRouche is featured on our website along with my remarks today.

LaRouche begins his discussion by stating that one of the biggest rules for conducting investigations, counterintelligence investigations particularly, is to highlight what *you don't know*—what might have happened that you missed. LaRouche says, "The most important events, among those you have overlooked, will usually be the non-events, events which never happened. The most important fact about a wedding is not the guest list or the bride's costume, but the fact that the groom is missing." Otherwise, he says in that paper, that any sound investigation must use the methods of Poe and Gauss and Kepler to map the axioms determining how populations and individuals think and react, and to determine as an organizer how you will intervene to get people to think differently, to free up their creativity. The method of thinking described in this paper is antithetical to the Internet and our present manipulated universe of public opinion, which traps us into profiled actions and reactions, into operating within fixed limits of thinking in the present—a universe in which profiled opinions are the dominant forces and the term "scientific truth" is not something that is ever really found. The divisions which so many declaim and say are a dominant part of American culture today are really not of the character attributed to them. Rather, they are like the ancient Roman pantheon, where dearly held beliefs were allowed to exist so long as any notion of universal truth was banished from the discussion, and so long as the opinions expressed rendered those expressing them politically impotent.

LaRouche says in the paper that anyone who intelligently examines any social or political process should remember that things in themselves do not exist; only *transformations in physical space-time* exist. He instructs you to ignore syllogisms in the form of nouns. He says, never make a decision based on facts of the form A is B; a fact for you is never a fact unless it is a statement of a transitive verb, a precise description of a transformation in the physical space-time observed. "A" happened in the context of "B." Finally, he details how to do crucial experiments involving mapping the underlying axioms of both social culture and the physical universe as thought by different populations, to determine the possible pathways for their future actions.

So it is with respect to the coup and the *non-events* of declassification and the public flaying of Rod Rosenstein. If you noticed, the coup stopped being a major focus in Trump's messaging about a month ago. Trump came out of his meeting with Rosenstein obviously having received an account of the events in question, which he believed, and also obviously having received assurances about where the Mueller investigation is going. Whether that is true or not is yet to be seen. But, in that respect, as Joseph diGenova said in an interview last week, Trump is now in possession of what he needs to know about the coup; and if you think about it, so are you. It was launched from Britain for the geopolitical purpose of either forcing Trump into collusion with the British view of the world, or forcing him from office. There is ample evidence already in the public record which more than demonstrates that.

We did our job, as we always should, by being the strategically accurate catalyst—operating from the unique perspective provided by LaRouche over all these years, and issuing the clarion call to the Congress and the President as to who was doing this and why it was happening. That clarion call was picked up and followed, and a great deal has been learned since, about the greatest abuse of our intelligence services in American history. Trump now knows more than we do about the results of what has been found, and he will utilize what he knows appropriately. For example, if the Democrats do succeed in flipping the House and move for impeachment, Trump is now holding the cards to be played by the Executive Branch, including the Department of Justice. Moreover, as opposed to the media accounts, Trump is now fully confident in setting up further meetings with the Russians, and John Bolton is playing a role in moving this process forward.

Desperation of a Cornered Enemy

What we can say, definitively, is that certain events which have happened in the past month—the revival of the Skripal hoax, the Khashoggi murder, the Central American caravan, and now, the pipe bomb duds sent to prominent players in the coup by a low-life criminal and self-described male strip dance choreographer and promoter, Cesar Sayoc—reek of desperation; all of it aimed at stanching the President's momentum in the elections and deflecting attention from the criminal actions of the President's opponents, who were the very specific targets of the crazed Cesar Sayoc. If you think about it, the choice of the players this loser allegedly targeted with his non-exploding explosives, was designed to immunize essential players in the coup against the President and deflect from what they have been doing, at least as it is being played by the mighty Wurlitzer of our propaganda machine. These guys have managed to invent a new narrative, a new pulp fiction novel that says that Donald Trump's crudity and profanity caused the deranged actions of Cesar Sayoc, and that this low-life is typical of the "deplorables around the President."

You can't even say at this point, although it would be inviting, that Cesar Sayoc is a police informant, although he most certainly smells like one; only that he is clearly mentally unstable, borderline retarded, and trapped in the conspirophile land of the Internet—all of which can be ascertained by looking at his now defunct Twitter account. The mental instability and deficiencies and the Internet fixation are sufficient causes, in themselves, for someone of this profile to act out.

So, it really is up to anybody with a brain to get out and vote accordingly, to repudiate this last, most insane, and irrational propaganda ploy, to turn it against those perpetrating it and to organize others to take the same action. Ask your friends and neighbors: Do the fake news mavens really think that people aren't going to look at what George Soros or Tom Steyer have done

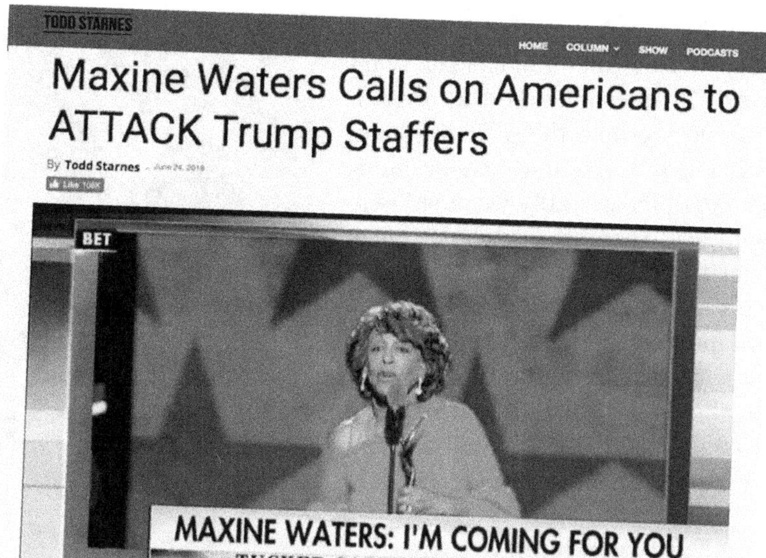

and only discuss it in the language of snowflakes because some deranged low-life and probable police informant was manipulated into violence? Most people now know that one out of every two people or more sitting next to them, except in certain bizarre locations on either Coast, support the President and are sane and rational human beings.

Now just think about the context and the midterms. The Kavanaugh hearings presented the American population with a full look at the descent into anarchy and hell and irrationality—the type of world they will face if the so-called Blue Wave is allowed to occur—and they reacted very strongly. In response to that reaction, a former Attorney General of the United States, Eric Holder, called for physically "kicking them while they are down," meaning Trump supporters. Hillary Clinton stared maniacally into a camera and threatened the population. She said, we can have civility if you give us back the House of Representatives. Finally, the *New York Times* ran an assassination fantasy story, with a Secret Service agent shooting the President—written, of course, by a Brit—the day before Cesar Sayoc's bombs started arriving. That's not to mention the antics of now "Mad Maxine" Waters or the sad and all used up figure of Al Green. So, these are desperate, desperate actions by an increasingly cornered British foe.

All of the events, cited above, as played by our media, are aimed at depressing the vote in the midterms. But it is also a fact that at this stage, the British ploy is losing its oxygen; it depends on insane events such as these for simple survival now. The Democrats completely overplayed their hand in the Kavanaugh hearings, striking at core features of the American identity: the presumption of innocence, due process, and fundamental fairness. The question before us today is how do we take the offensive now, rather than tolerating the continuing danger of the mortally wounded British beast? They have no choice but to fight to the end. They are staring at the very real possibility of historical collapse and jail for key actors. But if we win, what are we really winning if we allow this fight to be defined as it is being defined only right now in present time? Where are we, really?

The Future Determines the Present

Last week, LaRouche PAC released a mobilization statement for this election, emphasizing that we are really on the verge of making history for humanity—something you would not know if you allow your reality to be defined by current news events. We compared this moment to that of the lost chance of 1989 when the Berlin Wall fell and Franklin Roosevelt's intention of ending the British Empire once and for all was on the table. That opportunity was lost through British imperial perfidy and, most importantly, populations who thought small, and who failed to rise to the appropriate level of historical necessity.

At that time, the imperial elites promoted two versions of social control with which they experimented in the intervening period to maintain their power. One was fashioned as *neo-liberalism*, and is embodied in the doctrine of the so-called "end of history" by Francis Fukuyama. The other was fashioned as *neo-conservatism* as practiced by Dick Cheney and his crew of fascist Neanderthals, who sought to reshape the world by military force. Although the neo-conservatives crashed and burned with the Iraq War, they now are seeking a wholesale revival in the United States. As to the neo-liberalism embraced by Hillary Clinton and Barack Obama, Fukuyama himself says that it is the form of globalism embodied in the European Union and probably would not be accepted in the United States.

We pointed out that these twin—allegedly competing—ideologies concocted when the Wall fell, are just really different forms of *synarchism*—a synthetic political movement spawned by the European oligarchy which Franklin Roosevelt's intelligence units identified

Wikipedia

Barack Obama, presenting his Nobel lecture after receiving the Nobel Prize in 2009.

Gage Skidmore

Former Vice President Dick Cheney.

as Nazi-Communism. They are both a Satanic amalgam of Hegel, Nietzsche, Marx, Heidegger, and Kojève. It is no accident that Fukuyama later said that to really work, neo-liberalism had to include the complete abolition of technological breakthroughs and new scientific discoveries as essential features of his program. That is, mankind would have to be *permanently trapped in the present*, something which our present manipulated news cycle and Internet do actually accomplish. Add to that the myths about climate change, and you get Barack Obama lecturing Africans that their desire to live at a human level would destroy the planet because it would boil over.

Both these social control ideologies, neo-conservatism and neo-liberalism, have been smashed by Donald Trump and his call for reciprocally beneficial economic relationships between fully sovereign nation states. What is lacking now is something only the LaRouche movement can provide—an immediately actionable plan for the future which will work in the very short term, to create hope and prosperity in the wake of this destruction.

In our organizing, we have picked up the same thing the President picked up with respect to the public's perception of the coup. The American population is prepared to revolt from it, but really does not ache to have that battle in the context of present axioms, particularly as presented by "identity politics" at any level, or right and left political axioms and assumptions, or the present posture of either partisan political party, or even any present way of thinking.

The people we are talking to—disillusioned Democrats, independents, thinking Trump supporters, young people—are really concerned about the economic future: creating an economy which is not based on Wall

Street funny money; educating their children to be scientifically curious once again about the universe in which they find themselves; not relegated to such insane curricula as "gender studies," or endlessly playing video games and plunging into the fantasy of their phones. The people we meet demonstrate over and over again a yearning for bold thinking about the future. That is where our job is now. That is the path to saving this Presidency and saving the nation. That is really the end of the long national nightmare of our recent experience in the wake of the Bush and Obama presidencies.

We have already made substantial headway in this election through the Kesha Rogers campaign in Texas, through the messaging of John James for Senate in Michigan, in ending the plantation in which the Democrats have placed our most vulnerable populations. Ron Wieczorek is doing a similar job with the farm community. Now we have to expand that into the thinking about a higher future human culture, one which does not presently exist, which LaRouche began to explore in his "The Coming Eurasian World," and presenting it to a population thirsty for profound ideas.

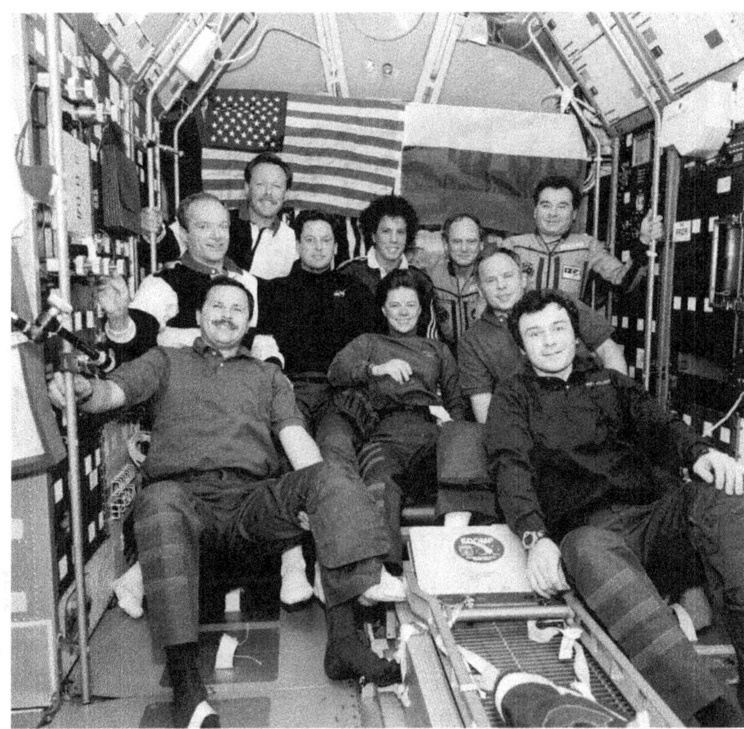

NASA

STA-71 and Mir 18 and Mir 19 crewmembers in the Spacelab module aboard Space Shuttle Atlantis *in the summer of 1995.*

Such a culture, as LaRouche imagined it, will have nothing to do with the boring homogeneity sought by Britain's social control professors, or the genetically based "diversity" presently inflaming our national debate. It is more like the experience of the International Space Station, where patriotic astronauts who love their countries and their cultures collaborate to discover and create new physical realities and new laws for the universe. That effort holds the immediate potential for large-scale economic development for all, and an end to capricious and completely immoral poverty.

The Victorious Flank

This new culture can only come into existence based on the Four Power Agreement which LaRouche specified for ending the rule of British Empire. It is only possible through stable long-term investment and credit mechanisms of a New Bretton Woods system based on sovereign nation states, endowed with full-set economies, developing the rest of the world while moving the platform for human culture to the space between the Earth and the Moon. Getting there requires thinking from the future back into the present, looking at events on Earth, as Bruce Director put it in his Thursday night Fireside Chat conference call, from the perspective of the astronaut in space. Similarly, borrowing another metaphor from Bruce's talk, the turbulence we are experiencing now can be seen, upon reflection, as like that turbulence associated with the initial flight which broke the sound barrier. As the breakthrough was approached, things got very, very turbulent. Once the plane went through the barrier, however, the flight was incredibly smooth and exhilarating.

And, if you are really surveying the entire domain, as LaRouche emphasizes in his "Cloak and Dagger" paper that I have referenced, you can see that this campaign of ours right now is absolutely urgent. The sword of Damocles in the form of looming economic collapse and war dominates the entirety of the present, if we continue to live in the intellectual universe of the present. This nation has been divided, not by Trump, but by years in which the search for truth was abandoned, and profiled emotion-laden opinions were substituted for thought. Fortunately, like the persons trapped by sense certainty in Edgar Allan Poe's masterful stories, the *Descent into the Maelstrom* or *The Pit and the Pendulum,* LaRouche's ideas and policies are there to rescue us, since the future always, lawfully, determines the present. And this is the victorious flank the enemy is really just incapable of imagining.

Thank you.

LaRouche Hamilton Candidates Campaign for the Future, and Defend the Presidency

by Dennis Speed

Oct. 30—The LaRouche PAC intervention into the 2018 mid-term elections, the Campaign to Secure the Future, has, from several indications, done what it set out to do, particularly in the form of the flagship Congressional candidacies of Kesha Rogers in Texas, and Ron Wieczorek in South Dakota. While support for, or opposition to the Trump Presidency is the apparent "dividing line" and "electoral flashpoint," something else entirely is afoot. A new set of policies, carrying the nation into the next half-century and beyond, is needed and available, and the Presidency of the United States needs to now act upon these policies in concert with Russia, China, and India. The President requires a cooperative Congress for that purpose, and there is no other sane choice before the American people than that.

There is another aspect to the domestic American political landscape. The media cannot afford to report it, or affirm it, so they stupidly pretend it does not exist. It is, that the economic reality lived by the 80-90% of politically disenfranchised Americans has impelled them, some-

EIRNS/Marsha Bowen

Kesha Rogers addresses a campaign concert at the Fort Bend Music Center in Stafford, Texas on Oct. 27.

times involuntarily, into emerging patterns of thought and behavior not seen in the United States since at least 1932, and perhaps not since the mid-nineteenth century. This process is in Classical political science termed a "mass strike" process, a little understood phenomenon that is the fundamental dynamic of social change in the post-American Revolutionary world.

Rogers and Wieczorek, basing their candidacies on the LaRouche Four Laws, are offering distinctly 21st/22nd Century solutions to this economic crisis. The Rogers campaign recently held a campaign event and concert in celebration of the 60th anniversary of the founding of the National Aeronautics and Space Administration (NASA), featuring not only meteorologist Tom Wysmuller, a former NASA employee, as a speaker, but also the candidate herself as a vocalist and soloist with a local chorus. In addition, 15 persons, including Rogers, joined 15,000 others in visiting the Johnson Space Center in Houston, which opened its doors to visitors for one day only, the first time in five years. Impor-

LPAC-TV

Tom Wysmuller, retired NASA meteorologist.

tantly, this was done not only in commemoration of the 60th anniversary of NASA, but the 20th anniversary of the International Space Station, showing that NASA views itself, and creative scientific discovery, as the natural bridge among all nations.

Campaign staff noted not only the large number of young people and families that were there, but the scientific optimism of all, most of whom were from the metropolitan Houston area. For years Rogers has relentlessly campaigned for an expansion of NASA, and collaboration with Russia, China, India and other nations in a Strategic Defense of Earth, and on crash programs for exploration and colonization of the Moon and near space. LaRouche's Fourth Law, promoting technologies based on new physical principles, implies a joint Moon-Mars mission, including the lunar mining of helium-3 to supply the fuel for fusion reactors, thus removing the physical necessity for dependence of all economies upon fossil fuels.

That new technological platform, however, demands that the Congressional district Rogers seeks to represent, and the city of Houston as a whole, become a "science driver" for the United States and a model for international collaboration, particularly in education. In the aftermath of the destruction of life and property in 2017, as a result of Hurricane Harvey, this optimistic educational perspective is sorely needed in the Ninth District, one of the poorest in the nation.

A Rogers staff member pointed out that "the Gemini and Apollo missions, Skylab, and the Space Shuttle flights were all supervised or coordinated out of the Johnson Space Center. Today it is part of the controlling and monitoring of the ISS [International Space Station]. It's one of the closest places on Earth to the Galaxy. So why isn't every child here thinking, not only about solving all the material problems confronting us on Earth, but of discovering new ways of thinking about the Solar system and the Galaxy? Sixty mil-

lion Chinese school kids watched their astronauts float weightless in space. They talked with them. They did experiments with them. NASA is looking at the Galaxy all the time. American children deserve to dream, and that's what our Campaign to Secure the Future is all about."

Dispossessed, Injured, Forgotten Farm Belt

Candidate Wieczorek, one of four running for South Dakota's single Congressional district, a farmer by profession for over 50 years, has been touring towns ranging from several hundred to a few thousand people—52 towns in a single four-day period, from early morning until very late at night. He and his volunteers are con-

EIRNS/Robert Baker

Ron Wieczorek addresses a campaign meeting in Sioux Falls, South Dakota on Oct. 14.

versing with people in those cafés, diners, and gas stations that still remain in the largely destroyed and closed centers of these once-growing, even prosperous towns. And the picture they are getting is of an America that is willfully unreported, and therefore unknown to other Americans. It has been dispossessed, injured and forgotten.

Associated with LaRouche for nearly four decades, Wieczorek vigorously supports a return to FDR's Glass-Steagall, the creation of a national credit system based on the U.S. Treasury, parity prices for farmers to encourage an expansion of family farms ("One million new farmers in the United States of America!") and the Chinese Belt and Road Initiative ("If China can do it, so can we!"). He has particularly taken on the "bullet-headed" idea, still prevalent in parts of South Dakota, that Russia is the primary enemy of the United States. Instead, Wieczorek insists: The primary enemy is the British Empire's "special relationship" with the United States, consisting of "so-called free trade," globalization, and "environmentalist" depopulation policies.

This has produced heated, even hostile confrontations. "But the difference," a 20-year-old volunteer from New York City reported, "is that people actually want to talk. People say that they have left the Republican *and* the Democratic Party, and they are looking for something else. They don't ignore you, like in New York. Even the knuckleheads want to know why we think that Russiagate is a hoax, and that Trump's policy of constructive engagement with Russia to stop war is right."

"Greedy-mean Al Green's" self-identification as "the voice of impeachment" from one of the poorest districts in the country, expresses the self-immolating dilemma of today's Democratic Party. Mortgaged to Soros, locked into defending the fully-exposed British Intelligence-directed illegal surveillance of Presidential candidates to fix the outcome of the U.S. elections, riddled with the disease of identity politics in the form of various "isms" and "phobias"—the Democratic Party has driven its once-loyal base to Independent or Republican candidates.

Disengagement from the "deplorable" 85% of Americans—voter base and all—in favor of a marijuana-fueled pipe dream of an environmentally sanitized, cooled-down, and globalized future, costing a mere $122 trillion dollars and about as likely to work as Adolf Hitler's "Thousand-Year Reich," would have once been seen as an unworkable campaign strategy. The Democratic Party leadership's blithe obliviousness to all this may be an unintentional clinical proof of the old observation that "pot smokers can't remember the brains they've lost."

Four-Power Agreement Trumps Impeachment

Four thousand people received, one by one, packages of Kesha Rogers literature at the October 22 rally held by Trump in Houston, in which about 45,000 people participated inside and outside. Five people called into a gospel radio station within two hours after the campaign's radio ads started to play, agreeing with the ad's criticisms of incumbent Congressman "Greedy Al" Green, and asking how to find out more about Rogers. About three hundred people have given their names to work with the campaign in the last seven days.

But what is it that these people are being organized to support? On South Dakota campuses, populated by an equal number of international students and locals, it has been the discussion of the needed dialogue among Putin, Trump, Xi Jinping, Prime Minister Modi of India, and other world leaders that has generated the greatest interest. A "New Bretton Woods" monetary system had some resonance among students familiar with what the 1944-1971 Bretton Woods system had been. Fifteen hundred students received leaflets, distributed one by one, over the past two weeks. Heated conversations about free trade, environmentalism, etc., occurred, but the idea of the heads of state of the four "continental nations" working together, as in the case of North Korea, to solve the world's problems, was met with receptivity and excitement. About ten percent of them indicated in various ways that they would continue contact with the campaign.

In 1856, the Republican Party fielded its first Presidential candidate. That party came about due to the failure of earlier political formations, and the inability of people to continue to support the Democratic Party, which was the party of slavery and treason. In 1932, President Franklin Delano Roosevelt, running as a Democrat, recruited posthumously the Republican Party's Abraham Lincoln to the Democratic Party. FDR reshaped that party in the image of Lincoln and George Washington, saving the souls of many of its leaders in the process. His New Deal for the American people, over the objections of Democratic Party boss and Wall Street tool John Jacob Raskob (a supporter of the 1933 Business plot to overthrow FDR, later exposed by Gen. Smedley Butler in Congressional testimony), is the same seismic change that is not only now required—it's now occurring.

Whether that change is led by candidates of the caliber of Kesha Rogers and Ron Wieczorek, and the policies that the 2018 Campaign to Secure the Future have successfully promulgated, depends on the intelligence and engagement of the American people in defense of the Presidency, and that Presidency's campaign against war, through a Four Powers dialogue.

Congressman Cornelius 'Neil' Gallagher

by Elliot Greenspan

Upon viewing a 2013 LaRouche PAC video documentary titled, *Profile in Courage: Congressman Neil Gallagher*, Lyndon LaRouche emphasized, "This helped to close the picture of the history of the United States from the time of the death of Franklin Roosevelt, until the present time.... Justice was never done on behalf of Mr. Gallagher, even though he was a servant of the nation in various capacities in the course of his lifetime."

Former U.S. Representative Cornelius "Neil" Gallagher passed away October 17 at the age of 97, after a long battle with brain cancer.

Neil Gallagher, as a leading member of Congress, was the only man alive who was not only a close personal friend of John F. Kennedy, but fought the apparatus associated with his assassination, that of his brother Robert F. Kennedy, and Martin Luther King.[1]

A Bayonne, New Jersey, Democrat serving in the House from 1959 to 1973, Congressman Gallagher was instrumental in bringing many elements of JFK's legislative agenda to fruition, including the creation of the Peace Corps and the Arms Control and Disarmament Agency. He was a key member of the House Committee on Foreign Affairs, chaired the Asia-Pacific Subcommittee, chaired the U.S.-Canadian Interparliamentary Committee, and was a U.S. delegate to the Nuclear Disarmament Committee. He was so influential in Congress that he was on Lyndon Johnson's short list for Vice President. He initiated an international battle against cancer through the United Nations, via a scientific dialogue between the United States and the Soviet Union.

He was reportedly most proud of his initiatives in India and in Congress to "stop the genocide as perpetrated by Pakistan against the East Bengalis (then East Pakistan)" in 1971; "his legislative actions saved millions of lives and paved the way for the creation of the sovereign state of Bangladesh."[2]

Schiller Institute Video

"I think the most important lesson is, if you have issue that's worthwhile going to war about, you better damn well have an army behind you."

But it was through Gallagher's creation in 1964 of a House Subcommittee on Privacy and Constitutional Rights, to investigate the rapid emergence of the "surveillance state," that he became a national leader—by exposing this treason, making it a burning national issue. And earning the hatred of J. Edgar Hoover, the first Director of the FBI.

Martin Luther King once wrote of Gallagher, "Here is a perennial warrior of penetrating intensity ... who does something about civil rights rather than merely talk about it." Author Ron Felber titled his book on the subject, *The Privacy War: One Congressman, J. Edgar Hoover, and the Fight for the Fourth Amendment*.

Gallagher's courage and tenaciousness in taking on the danger of this burgeoning Hooverite police-state apparatus led to a witch hunt against him, his frame-up,

---

1. The *Profile in Courage: Congressman Neil Gallagher* video-documentary, produced in 2013, is available on the LaRouche PAC website, and, in transcript form, in *EIR* Vol. 43, No. 9, Feb. 26, 2016. Readers are urged to watch the video, and hear much of this story from Gallagher himself. Most of the quotes here are from that documentary.

2. Much of the biographical material here, as this quote on Bangladesh, comes from Ron Felber's biography, *The Privacy War: One Congressman, J. Edgar Hoover, and the Fight for the Fourth Amendment*. Our thanks to Mr. Felber for his extraordinary report on this history.

jailing and removal from Congress. The journalist Anthony Summers, in a book on Hoover, described this as "the most savage attack on a government official in the twentieth century."

Go back to April 1945. A decorated war hero, with three Purple Hearts, Neil Gallagher was just out of an army hospital after six months recovering from his wounds. He was reassigned to the position of honor guard for President Roosevelt in Hyde Park, New York. The honor guard did not serve, however, because on April 12, FDR died.

Gallagher, Boggs Expose 'Secret Government'

The historic enemy of the United States, the British Empire, and the Empire's American assets—Truman, Joe McCarthy, the Dulles brothers, Hoover, et al.—attacked the FDR legacy, and any leader committed to the policies of FDR and the Hamilton-Lincoln-FDR "American System." Gallagher's friend, President Kennedy, was such a leader. In the LaRouche PAC video-interview, Gallagher said that "Kennedy gave hope to the young people. And all of the people around the world who had fought in the war [World War II], it was our turn to be on the stage. He truly was a leader of the world's hope." The Anglo-American genocidalists set out to crush that hope.

In the wake of the assassination of the President, and the Warren Commission cover-up, with a British-instigated colonial war escalating in Vietnam, with anti-war and civil rights upheavals building to a crescendo in the late-1960s, the Hooverite police-state capability massively expanded. The Anglo-American intelligence apparatus intended to control the Presidency and the Congress, and to impose a new paradigm of cultural pessimism on a shocked and demoralized population.

Gallagher fought this on several fronts, proceeding from his core commitment to fight injustice, and to protect individual freedom. Years before, as a Hudson County Freeholder, he refused to sponsor Sen. Joseph McCarthy at a communion breakfast at his Bayonne church. "I hated everything McCarthy stood for. I had an innate feeling against injustice and he was one of the worst provocateurs of injustice in those days."

When confronted in Congress with Government injustice—intrusion into private lives, massive use of polygraphs, clandestine surveillance, illegal wiretapping and monitoring—Gallagher held hearings to expose this. He began to investigate and expose the evil

"I worry very much about what the hell's going to happen to this country, unless people become aware of [the secret government]." Here Congressman Gallagher is shown with John Kennedy and Lyndon Johnson, in the 1960s.

of the "secret government" within the Government. The response was explosive: His first hearing generated 28,000 letters from American citizens about Government abuse. He was named Chairman of a new special House Subcommittee on Privacy and Constitutional Rights, which held dozens of hearings. Among his achievements was the passage of the Freedom of Information Act in 1966, and the defeat of a plan for a computerized National Data Bank.

This brought him into a head-to-head confrontation with J. Edgar Hoover, and Hoover's FBI "National Gestapo." At the time, Hoover was deploying his police-state operation to destroy Bobby Kennedy and Dr. King, and demanded Gallagher's help. Gallagher refused, and Hoover attempted to terrorize him, as he terrorized most of Congress—through surveillance, intimidation, blackmail and more. But, as Gallagher's daughter said at his funeral, "He was fearless."

In a March 1970, New Jersey speech, the Congressman warned, "Never before in our history, has the group of basic concepts embodied in the first Ten Amendments to our Constitution, been under such constant and concerted attack as now.... We are in the process of losing our form of Government and our way of life, as it has developed since the founding of our Republic." He compared this to the unfolding of totalitarianism in Europe. "The ruination of individual privacy has always heralded the destruction of human freedom ... as with Hitler."

In the LaRouche PAC interview, Gallagher remarks

that "In those days, the only two [Congressmen] who were really battling Hoover were Hale Boggs and myself." Members of Congress became more and more aware that they were under surveillance, forcing legislators to meet with Gallagher in secret. "Hoover was a cancer to this country and a cancer to the Congress. You talk about behavioral modification, Hoover modified the behavior of the Congress."

In 1968, Gallagher was uncovering the most damning secrets. His investigations went into Government programs for behavior modification, hypnosis and other forms of "drugging and modification of the mind, to make more perfect assassins and spies." He, Boggs, New Orleans District Attorney Jim Garrison, and others, were on the "trail of the assassins."

By early 1971, Majority Leader Boggs called for Hoover's resignation on the floor of the House: "When the FBI taps the telephones of members of this body, and the Senate, when it stations agents on campuses, when the FBI adopts the tactics of the Soviet Union and Hitler's Gestapo, it is way past time to demand his resignation." Boggs' mission, to bring down Hoover, was in parallel with his attempt to reopen the investigations of the assassinations of the Kennedys and King.

Secret Government Strikes Back

Soon thereafter, in April 1971, Gallagher's Invasion of Privacy Committee was shut down. He drafted a bill to create a permanent committee. Hoover blackmailed Congress to block it. "That was the last attempt to set up any kind of a permanent committee that would consider the impact of the new technology on the civil liberties of the American people and their civil rights."

In April 1972, a federal grand jury indicted Gallagher on conspiracy, perjury and Federal income tax evasion. Gallagher went to the floor of the Congress, and for the first time there, put forward the details of the filth thrown at him from Hoover, the intimidation of Congress, and the incredible revelations that had been presented to his subcommittee regarding U.S. Army, FBI, and CIA abuses of Constitutional rights against Americans. He called for Hoover's resignation or firing. Two weeks later, Hoover died, mysteriously. (Years

Schiller Institute Video

earlier, at the height of Hoover's fabricated smears against Gallagher for alleged ties to the mafia, and worse, luridly published in *Life* magazine, the Congressman told Hoover stooge Roy Cohn, "I will drive that old bastard into a heart attack....")

Seven months later, in October 1972, a plane carrying Hale Boggs disappeared in Alaska. Gallagher describes his response in the LaRouche PAC video:

I always thought they blew the plane up. Because Hale was starting to make a lot of noise, like I did, although he was a more serious guy, because he had been on the Warren Commission. He wanted to re-open the Warren Commission, and then the plane mysteriously blew up. And those guys were not against things like that.

Did somebody blow up his goddamned plane? Why not! They couldn't shut him up! They shut me up! They dismembered my seat in the Congress, they indicted me, [but] there was never any corruption or payoffs or bribes, or anything. The Judge said that, but they gerrymandered me out of Congress, and soon to jail.

"They" did not quite shut him up. He carried forward this war for civil liberties and constitutional rights virtually to his death. He lectured in colleges, wrote and published widely about the degradation of privacy and the dramatic growth of the "surveillance state." His fight was portrayed in books and movies and documentaw0ries. Congressional investigations echoed his, and Boggs', wars. He had so earned the "undying enmity" of the "secret government," that a nine-year FBI-IRS-ATF- DEA surveillance/investigation of Gallagher and much of his family culminated in a huge raid on his home in 1992, and a second jailing in 1996.

Neil Gallagher Meets Lyndon LaRouche

At a 2013 New Jersey gubernatorial campaign event for LaRouche PAC candidate Diane Sare, Gallagher hammered at the "Secret Government ... the NSA and over 70 secret police agencies victimizing the American public." A kind of "Dialogue of Heroes" ensued at the event with Lyndon LaRouche, who cited "a certain, special kind of affinity, because of what we've gone through, as well as our relative ages." In fact, soon after his 17 months in jail, in 1973-74, the former Congressman met the LaRouche movement, subscribed to *Executive Intelligence Review*, and engaged in a 40-year dialogue with associates of Lyndon LaRouche.

In 1995, he joined 500 current and former elected officials internationally in a *Washington Post* ad calling for LaRouche's exoneration. Often accompanied by vigorous debate, Neil Gallagher voiced his support for many policy initiatives, including the current LaRouche PAC campaign for a New Bretton Woods monetary system.

"I gave it a try." Gallagher said in the 2013 LaRouche PAC video:

> I gave it a try, and I smashed my whole career as a result of it. And I'm not sorry! Because, what the hell would be the sense of staying down there, not being able to look in the mirror, or anything. I think the overall picture, of the emerging of the secret-police apparatus in America, which really came to a head with the Kennedy assassination, is, today, bigger and stronger than ever.
>
> You don't really have a Hoover around today, but you have a heck of a lot of guys with the power that Hoover had, who are a little more quiet and a little more efficient in the exercise of that kind of power.
>
> I worry very much about what the hell's going to happen to this country, unless people become aware of it. The frailty of civilization, and the ability to destroy it is so widespread now. As long as people in the Congress don't raise these questions about the role of the secret government in America, or the secret 'governments' in America, or the real role of the secret societies in America—as long as there's no protection for them, they can be destroyed overnight.... Now it breaks your heart. It breaks your heart, since you see what has to be done, what *should* be done, what Congress as a whole could do, but can't do any more. I think the most important lesson is, if you have an issue that's worthwhile going to war about, you better damn well have an army behind you. I didn't.

Congressman Neil Gallagher

LaRouchePAC has produced a 100-minute video interview, which digs up long-buried and forgotten secrets, presented in the voice of one individual who was at the center of the dramatic events of the 1950s, '60s, and early '70s, the period of the Joe McCarthy/J. Edgar Hoover witchhunts; the assassinations of John F. Kennedy, Robert Kennedy, and Martin Luther King, and much more. That individual, former New Jersey Congressman Cornelius Gallagher (1959-73) tells the story of those events, in which he paid a high price for his courage.

www.larouchepac.com/node/4544

The IPCC's 'Very Big Political Agenda' Is Human Extinction

by Stanley Ezrol

Oct. 27—President Donald Trump, at the outset of his historic "60 Minutes" interview with ageing nag Lesley Stahl, became the first major world leader, aside from Lyndon H. LaRouche, Jr., to refute the scientific validity of the "climate change" hoax represented by the Intergovernmental Panel on Climate Change (IPCC), promoted by the global financial establishment, and endorsed by every major national government on the planet. He pointed out, as we all used to learn in school, and as every climate scientist knows, that it is true that the climate has been constantly changing throughout history.

Trump attacked the totally unsupported IPCC claim that suddenly, since some time about a century ago, climate change, which had been going on for billions of years before the appearance of the first creative human beings, is now something that human beings must be eliminated to correct. This is no exaggeration.

One of the leading figures pushing the IPCC agenda is John Schellnhuber, an adviser to the German government and the Vatican on climate change, whom Queen Elizabeth named a Commander of the British Empire (CBE). At the 2009 Copenhagen climate conference, he announced that the "carrying capacity" of the Earth was less than one billion human beings, meaning that 6.5 billion or more of us must be eliminated.

Various studies have debunked the Climate Change agenda, item by item. A group

consciousnachhaltigkeit2009.commerzbank.de

Hans Joachim Schellnhuber, Commander of the British Empire, promoter of population-reducing policies in the name of defending against "climate change."

of NASA scientists and engineers, "The Right Climate Stuff," regularly posts materials and presents lectures in an effort to separate NASA from fraudulent materials on climate change. Simply, the IPCC contention is that of all of the factors—for instance, the vast power of the Sun—that affect our climate, the only one that counts is the slight variations in the carbon dioxide content of the atmosphere which is approximately 0.04%. On top of the insanity of that, they further contend that the 3% of that 0.04% (0.0012%) that humans have produced is what counts, and that the 97% produced by "nature" means nothing. They expect you to believe this without any data at all to demonstrate that this has ever been the case or ever could be the case, because they are experts.

When Trump pointed out, "We have scientists that disagree with that," Stahl demonstrated the utter mindlessness of those who do agree, by asserting that the fact that there were hurricanes and that glaciers were melting in Greenland should cause Trump to say, "I've changed my mind. There really is climate change"—which we are supposed to understand means "human beings are causing world-threatening changes to the climate." Trump responded simply, "And you don't know whether or not that would have happened with or without man. You don't know." When Stahl claimed that there are scientists "who say that it's worse than ever," Trump requested her to bring them forward because, "They have a very big political agenda."

The Climate Change Political Agenda is Human Extinction

Trump was, perhaps, more truthful than he realizes. The Climate Change agenda is in the millennia-old tradition of those tyrants who seek to protect their "birthright" from common humans. These useless, mega-consuming lords have never understood productive physical or cognitive labor, and so they see those who engage in it as competitors for resources which they do not understand how to produce.

The January 11, 1960 *Time* magazine cover story, "The Population Explosion," was one high-profile element in the launching of population control as a dominant factor in twentieth-century culture. This author, as a fifth grader at the time, recalls examining the theory of the piece and concluding, "Of course people eat food and use other things, but everything we have is made by people. How do we get anything if we don't have people to make it?" His views have developed since then, especially since he encountered Lyndon H. LaRouche, Jr., in 1972. Unfortunately, the "leaders" of modern culture have slipped further behind.

The now fallen, self-imagined King of Olympus, Al Gore, was once a prominent leader in this decline of civilization. Gore, the only individual in history to have won both an Oscar and the Nobel Peace Prize—the Peace Prize was shared with the IPCC; the Oscar was not—for the same piece of garbage, has now fallen from grace due to his own disgusting appetites, but his ideas, sadly, live on. Gore is in the British liberal tradition of Bertrand Russell and his collaborator Julian Huxley, which can be summarized as "Obey the King. Forget everything else, especially the future requirements of humanity." In his 1992 book, *Earth in the Balance*, Gore summarized his support for Zeus against Prometheus:

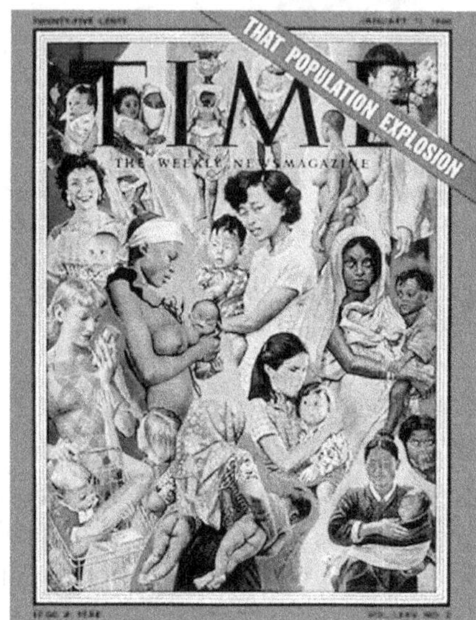

We have also fallen victim to a kind of technological hubris, which tempts us to believe that our new powers may be unlimited.... In a modern version of the Greek myth, our hubris tempts us to appropriate for ourselves—not from the gods but from science and technology—awesome powers and to demand from nature godlike privileges to indulge our Olympian appetite for more. Technological hubris tempts us to lose sight of our place in the natural order and believe that we can achieve whatever we want.

At the root of this belief lies a heretical misunderstanding of humankind's place in the world as old as Plato, as seductive in its mythic appeal as Gnosticism, as compelling as the Cartesian promise of Promethean power—and it has led to tragic results. We have misunderstood who we are, how we relate to our place within creation, and why our very existence assigns us a duty of moral alertness to the consequences of what we do.

Creative Commons/Tom Raftery

Al Gore gives a keynote address on sustainability at SapphireNow 2010, in May 2010.

The Greek myth Gore refers to is the story of the imperial Zeus, who resolved to eliminate his creation, humanity, from existence because it was becoming too powerful and too knowledgeable. Prometheus, whose promise Gore charges "has led to tragic results," stood against Zeus and rescued humankind by providing it with the knowledge, not only of fire (energy production), but of the full range of arts and sciences.

Fifteen years later, to make sure no one forgot whose side he was on, Gore published a much more succinct book, *The Assault on Reason*, in which he attacked our society for independently making scientific judgments, rather than following the "experts' advice" as Trump refused Lesley Stahl's request that he do. The IPCC has

President Barack Obama, speaking at the University of Johannesburg's Soweto Campus, June 29, 2013.

never repudiated its Peace Prize partner, so we must assume that they accept his judgment that they must be believed simply because they are "the experts" and they say so. The nations of the world and all of their great educational institutions have backed the IPCC policy despite their failure to provide any other reason why they should be believed.

Obama's Horrible Dreams

A currently leading follower of "the experts" on "climate change" is ex-President Barack Obama. On June 29, 2013, addressing his own creation, the Young African Leaders Initiative Town Hall at the University of Johannesburg-Soweto in Johannesburg, South Africa, Obama pronounced a death sentence against the young people he had assembled.

> Ultimately, if you think about all the youth that everybody has mentioned here in Africa, if everybody is raising living standards to the point where everybody has got a car and everybody has got air conditioning, and everybody has got a big house, well, the planet will boil over—unless we find new ways of producing energy. And tomorrow, or the next day, when I visit Tanzania, I'm actually going to be going to a power plant to focus on the need for electrification, but the need to do it in an environmentally sound way.

Think of Obama as Zeus, explaining to his human creatures why they all must die. Imagine yourself, perhaps as Prometheus, deciding exactly what you must do about it. Obama had, and has, no intention of finding "new ways of producing energy." He has been a militant opponent of nuclear energy, the only "environmentally sound" energy technology available that can do the job. The "Power Africa" project Obama went to visit in Tanzania has emphasized household solar energy production along with biomass, natural gas, and other carbon-burning fuels that fail the "clean energy" test. None of these are adequate to meet the massive industrial development requirements of the 1.3 billion Africans now faced with early deaths from disease, malnutrition, a lack of potable water, and the resulting conflicts caused by the cowardly surrender by the great nations of the world to "the experts."

Now is the time to set things right. Though not explicitly challenging the IPCC, China and her collaborators are committed to expanding nuclear power production and other advanced technologies. Trump has shown he is willing to brush aside the demand that he kiss the experts—anywhere. Learn what you have to. There is real science, and we should all get accustomed to thinking critically and scientifically, but the IPCC is the very wrong stuff.

Fuqing Nuclear Power Plant, No. 5 unit, in China's Fujian Province. The containment dome installation was completed May 25, 2017. China's first demonstration nuclear power project using Hualong One technology, a domestically developed third-generation reactor design.

The IPCC Global Warming Report and Drug Legalization Moves in South Africa

by Ramasimong Phillip Tsokolibane, leader of LaRouche South Africa

Oct. 29—I want to draw your immediate and urgent attention to two policy matters that—while the fake news and fake commentators treat them as separate items—are most directly related and must be rejected, for their murderous intent. When we speak of murder, especially on a grand scale of the type referred to as genocide, I must insist that we are usually speaking of the policy the British Empire, and the Queen that rules it, along with her consort, His Royal Virus, Prince Philip, and their Dumbo-eared dolt of a son, Charles.

The IPCC Report is a Cover for Genocide

Last month, the Intergovernmental Panel on Climate Change (IPCC) issued a report that once again blamed the human race for what it claimed was the impending collapse of the Earth's eco-systems, caused by alleged global warming. It then demanded that the nations of the world commit themselves to drastic reductions in productive human activity, so as to limit the projected global warming, caused by human-caused carbon emissions, to 1.5°C. This message was immediately spread around the globe by the fake news outlets.

Let me state emphatically: *There is no basis in real science for the IPCC's fear mongering!* Real science shows, as former NASA scientist Tom Wysmuller so eloquently explained recently to a meeting of the LaRouche movement's Manhattan Project in New York City, the so-called "facts" to support the case, as represented by graphics, don't support the IPCC arguments about either the reality of global warming or its alleged cause. Human activity, including all production, is not even a *significant factor* in causing climate change, and

reductions in that activity would have little or no real effect on what they allege is happening.

But the deeper issue, as also expressed by the IPCC, is its neo-Malthusian argument, that when all is said and done, there are simply too many people on the planet. Their "final solution" to the phony problem that they have hyped is to reduce the world's population to around 1 billion people, or less. This is the true content of the environmentalists' propaganda, whose lunacy has unfortunately infected and brainwashed the minds of frightened people, even here in Africa. This is a call for support for the greatest genocide in history, one that would have made the British-installed golem, Adolf Hitler, blush with envy.

Creative Commons/Roberta Bocchese

Queen Elizabeth and Prince Philip.

While global warming is a hoax, no matter how loud the fake news and various enviro-jerks scream otherwise, the effects of following the policies proposed by the neo-Malthusians—slowing down and halting the pace of development of the type envisioned by the BRICS nations and China's Belt and Road Initiative, slowing or halting plans to electrify Africa and the rest of the Global South, halting the peaceful use of nuclear energy—these effects will be very real and very drastic indeed. Such policies will bring death to billions of human beings—the population reduction desired by His Royal Virus Prince Philip and the other leaders of the British-inspired environmental movement.

I have said this before, but it needs restating: Let no African be confused—whenever you hear talk of killing billions, know that it will begin with you and me. That has always been the Empire's way. We are the ones who are slated to die, as are others in Central and

South America, and in Asia. But not just there. Europe will lose population, as will the United States, by the millions, and it won't be only "people of color."

Ironically, the man whom the fake media tries to portray as a racist, the American President Donald Trump, is perhaps our last, best hope for saving humanity from these genocidal lunatics. He has refused, so far, to cave in to the screeches for reduced economic activity and development; he has refused, so far, to believe that cutting back advanced economic activity is a solution to anything. For this he has been excoriated, as has Lyndon LaRouche before him, for daring to oppose phony environmentalist science. But Trump has not yet dared, as LaRouche has done, to lay the source of this evil squarely at the feet of the British Empire.

While many have cited George Soros, the billionaire speculator, as one of the principal funding supporters of the global environmental movement and the global warming hoax, they fail to understand that Soros was created by, and serves his master, the British Empire, which created the modern environmentalist movement. Following President Trump's statement about climate change in a recent interview, "I don't know that it's man-made," Megan Beets of the LaRouche PAC Science Research Team and Tom Wysmuller, a retired NASA meteorologist, presented a strong refutation of the latest IPCC report that calls for drastic reductions of man-made carbon dioxide. Megan Beets proves that the world needs more people, not less, while Tom Wysmuller demonstrates the claim of alarming increases of the ocean level is a lie.[1]

As the LaRouche movement exposed more than three decades ago, the British created the neo-Malthusians, who gathered around such swarms of evil maggots as the Club of Rome and Prince Philip's own World Wildlife Fund (now the Worldwide Fund for Nature, WWF), whose Panda symbol became the mark of the new beastman movement; its minions have locked up millions of acres of Africa's sovereign land in game preserves, transformed into playgrounds for the hunter bwanas among the world's 1%'ers, while blocking comprehensive development projects that might help the rest of us survive.

Among the major funders of the WWF and the once prominent Club of Rome (promoters of the phony "Limits to Growth" of decades past, whose Malthusian logic has been reborn in the reports of the IPCC) are the big oil companies, such as Royal Dutch Shell and British Petroleum, who become richer by far by *limiting* the use of hydrocarbon fuels, while blocking nuclear power, and delaying and underfunding the development of fusion power, a potentially unlimited and cheap source of energy championed by LaRouche and his international movement.

Constitutional Court Legalizes Marijuana

But consider also a seemingly unrelated development: On Sept. 18, in a unanimous ruling, South Africa's highest court, the Constitutional Court, legalized the use of cannabis by adults in private places, as well as the growing of marijuana for private consumption. That ruling paves the way for the full legalization of the sale and use of marijuana, by stating that the current laws that prohibit its use violate the constitution.

First, the move to legalize dagga and other illicit drugs is part of a global movement, funded by the same British asset, George Soros, so heavily involved in funding the global warming hysteria. One nation after another is succumbing to these British bankers' drugging movement, which most recently claimed Canada as a victim.

Die for the British Empire or Save Yourself with LaRouche, BRICS and BRI

Second, I shall tell you that the move to keep people stoned and high on drugs, goes hand in hand with the effort to organize a global genocide. If you are smoking dope, you will be less likely to oppose the plans for the global genocide implicit in Global Warming hoax and required to comply with the IPCC report. In fact, the people who support the IPCC and similar organizations and their warnings, are a confluence of pot smokers. "Keep 'em high, and let them die," the Queen says.

I urge all of you who don't want to die at the hands of the British Empire to oppose these twin evils—the IPCC report and the drive to make dope legal—by joining with me and the movement I represent in separating our nation and all of humanity from the clutches of the British Empire. Support my fight to align our nation further with the emerging new paradigm as represented by the policies and institutions of the BRICS, of which South Africa is a proud member, and of China's Belt & Road Initiative (BRI). We owe no allegiance to any crown, but to the common welfare and future of humanity.

If you wanna be high, you're going to die—as the British Queen intends. There are no limits to growth other than the dope-infused ideology of the British Empire and its Wall Street satrapy.

---

1. See https://larouchepac.com/20181020/global-warming-population-reduction-not-science

The World Needs More People!

This is an edited presentation by Megan Beets to the Oct. 20, 2018 Manhattan Project meeting in New York City. A video of the full meeting may be found here.

Megan Beets: On October 8 of this year, about two weeks ago, the UN's IPCC—the Intergovernmental Panel on Climate Change—released a new report, which demands that nations cut back even more on industrialization, and that nations make even greater efforts to curb and cut population growth. This IPCC demand is premised on its fraudulent insistence that we have to limit the average rise of global temperatures not to two degrees Celsius, but to 1.5 degrees Celsius. This, as I'm going to go through, is based on a complete lie; it has nothing to do with science. You've all heard this claim that 99 point-something percent of scientists now agree that human beings are causing cataclysmic climate change on the planet with our greedy industrial policies—and, therefore, that we have to stop development. You've all heard that!

This isn't science. Whatever those poor scientists were roped into, this has nothing to do with science. This is the policy of Empire, and I'm going to go through that today.

Why is this coming up now? Why are they so desperate? In 2016 when Donald Trump won the Presidential election, the next morning Lyndon LaRouche said:

This is not a local United States phenomenon; this is a global phenomenon. What you're seeing are signs of breakdown of what's been a decades-long paradigm of globalization, of geopolitics, and of empire. The empire system is crumbling.

LaRouche said we have to mobilize not just the American people, but the world's population to bring into being a New Paradigm. We'll talk a little bit at the

A view of Earth taken by the crew of the Apollo 17 spacecraft, Dec. 7, 1972.

end about what that should look like.

The biggest sickness that has taken over is a mentality of anti-growth, anti-development, anti-progress. That is what we have to break. This starts with crushing the brainwashing that's taken over schools, it's taken over TV commercials, it absolutely pervades the culture. We have to crush the idea that the world is over-populated. Not only is that not true, the world is vastly under-populated. Not just from the standpoint of what we could support given today's level of technology, but also from the standpoint of what we as a human species need to get done over the next two generations. We don't have enough people on Earth to do that, and we've got to get to work!

Does anybody know what the current world population is? It's about 7.6 billion people. What's the right level of population? What should the world have? Ten billion? Is that enough? Twenty?

Audience Member: You say the Earth is not over-populated, so maybe it should be at least double that?

Beets: OK, 15 billion people, something like that? Let's take a look at what Lyndon LaRouche said would be a good starting point:

Lyndon LaRouche: [video] That is, if we were to take the attitude which the United States had under the Kennedy space program, or it was actually the Eisenhower-Kennedy space program, from about 1958 the so-called post-Sputnik program, to about 1965. If we maintain that, with policies of tax investment credits for productive investments, combined with science-enrichment programs in our schools and similar kinds of things that we did then; nothing more than that. I can assure you, that knowing what we know is important to work upon in science, in technology, knowing the kinds of projects that will best express these technological improvements. I assure you that if mankind on this planet had the political will

UNESCO

Julian Huxley

to do that, we would increase the potential population density on this planet, at a higher standard of living, by a factor of as much as 40 over that of today. In the next three generations, by a factor of ten. By the end of two generations, we would be sustaining a potential population in the order of magnitude of 100 billion people more comfortably, much better fed, much more secure, much freer, much less crowded than today.

Beets: So, is 100 billion too much? Imagine what kind of world that implies. One hundred billion people living longer, healthier, more fulfilling lives; much less crowded, with cleaner air than what we enjoy today. What will humanity have become were we to achieve that? And is that possible?

I want to take it back to where this anti-development, anti-human, pro-colonial attitude and movement came from. What are its roots? Does anybody know what the problem was that the British faced when World War II was drawing to a close? What was their biggest fear? Anybody know?

Audience Member: That they were taken over by the U.S. Empire.

Beets: Yes! Throughout the course of World War II, Franklin Roosevelt made it clear to Winston Churchill, that after the war, the post-war system would not be a reconstruction of colonialism. Now, Roosevelt died at

the end of the war, but that was the fear; that the post-war system was going to be a modern system of nation-states where the people in the nation were allowed to use their own resources for their own development. And that every person in the world should enjoy a high and equal standard of living; the highest possible standard of living. This terrified the British Empire.

British Eugenics

After the war, an ideology was developed, supported, and peddled by the British—one that had earlier been put on grand display by Hitler in the genocidal policies carried out by the Nazi regime—namely, the ideology of eugenics. Race "science." Culling the herd to produce the "master race" of humanity. This was a creation of the British. This became a little bit of an unpopular idea, following what happened in Germany in World War II. So, the British got to work, and they rebranded eugenics as "ecology" and "conservationism." One of the founders of the ecology movement was Julian Huxley. I want to read a quote of Julian Huxley. Huxley was the first chairman of UNESCO—the United Nations Educational, Scientific, and Cultural Organization. In its 1946 founding document, Huxley wrote:

> Thus, even though it is quite true that any radical eugenic policy will be for many years politically and psychologically impossible, it will be important for UNESCO to see that the eugenic problem is examined with the greatest care, and that the public mind is informed of the issues at stake, so that much that what now is unthinkable may at least become thinkable.

Two years later, in the launching of the ecology and conservation movement, Huxley wrote: "The spread of man must take second place to the conservation of other species."

There's a lot to say about Huxley which we don't have time for, but in the 1930s, Huxley helped found an organization in Britain called Political and Economic Planning (PEP), which promoted the kind of fascist economic policies that were taken up by Mussolini. Huxley also worked with the British Eugenics Society, of which he was both a member and later the head, to found two organizations in Britain—the Population Policy Committee and the Royal Commission on Population, both of which produced studies about the horrible effects of population growth on resources.

Another great proponent of the "ecology" movement was Lord Bertrand Russell. Let's take a look at what Russell thought about the human species. In 1951, he wrote a book called *The Impact of Science on Society*, in which he said:

> Bad times, you may say, are exceptional and can be dealt with by exceptional methods. This has been more or less true during the honeymoon period of industrialism, but it will not remain true unless the increase of population can be enormously diminished. At present the population of the world is increasing at about 58,000 per diem. War, so far, has had no very great effect on this increase, which continued through each of the world wars.... War ... has hitherto been disappointing in this respect ... but perhaps bacteriological war may prove more effective. If a Black Death could spread throughout the world once every generation, survivors could procreate freely without making the world too full.... The state of affairs might be somewhat unpleasant, but what of it? Really high-minded people are indifferent to happiness, especially other people's.

This is not an uncommon attitude. You find the exact same genocidal desire expressed, for example, by the Royal Consort, Prince Philip, who expressed his wish to be reincarnated as a deadly virus so that he could contribute something to solving over-population. This is a genocide policy; no question about it.

Royal Game Preserves and Depopulation

In 1960, Huxley traveled—when he was in his sixties—throughout Africa for several months. Upon his return, Huxley wrote a number of articles which basically said that these newly independent African nations cannot be trusted with the protection of natural spaces and endangered species. Therefore, we must have an international body which can take stewardship of these lands.

He followed up on that, and in 1961, Huxley—along with Prince Philip and Max Nicholson, who was the head of the Queen's Privy Council—founded the World Wildlife Fund. Incidentally, Prince Philip was not the first head of the World Wildlife Fund. In order to make it appear a bit distant from the British Royal family, they asked Prince Bernhard of the Netherlands to be the first head of the World Wildlife Fund. Unfortunately, Prince Bernhard was a former card-carrying Nazi, who signed his Nazi Party resignation letter with "Heil Hitler!" But that's the pedigree of this thing. So, the World Wildlife Fund was founded in 1961 by eugenics supporters and former Nazis.

I want to read a quote from Max Nicholson. It's important, but also for what happens at the end; because that will give you some perspective on what we are being subjected to today. So, Nicholson, co-founder of the World Wildlife Fund, said:

> We should perhaps look back as far as the Reformation and the Renaissance for a comparable general disintegration of long settled values and patterns through the impact of new outlooks and new ideas. [Just to be clear, the long settled values and patterns he seeks to disrupt are the idea that man is a co-creator, the

Bertrand Russell

Duke of Edinburgh Prince Philip (left) and Prince Bernhard of the Netherlands in Amsterdam, Netherlands, in 1967.

idea that human beings are good, and the idea that human progress is good. —MB]

The message and beliefs will be a kind of seismic upheaval which is bound to leave in its train heaps of intellectual and ethical rubble. *Seismic seems the right word because the emotional force and intensity behind the idea of conservation is as important as its intellectual power.*

So, whipping people up is as important, or even more important, than telling the truth in this matter.

By the mid-1990s, the World Wildlife Fund had gained control of nearly 2 million square kilometers of land in Africa. That's about 8 percent of the entire African continent!—which was cordoned off and turned into wildlife preserves, denying all access to those nations for the development of their people. The World Wildlife Fund has not just done this on the continent of Africa; it's done this in Central America, in South America, in South Asia. A good example is the Darién Gap, which is the connection point between the North American and South American continents, which to this day has no transportation link across it— to this day. The reason is, it's a giant nature preserve of the WWF.

That was 1961. Throughout the 1960s and 1970s, in the wake of the trauma from the assassination of John F. Kennedy and the ramping up of the Vietnam War, there was a full-on onslaught against the developing nations. For example, in 1962, you had the publication of a seminal work called *Silent Spring*. Has anybody heard of this? *Silent Spring* was a book by Rachel Carson, which claimed that human beings are poisoning the planet.

Case in point: DDT, which is the most effective pesticide against mosquitoes and other disease-carrying insects. Carson claimed that DDT was thinning the eggshells of birds, and therefore must be banned. This claim was based on scientific experiments which were very quickly redone and all proven to be false. Yet, DDT to this day is banned. The banning of DDT has led to at least, conservatively, the unnecessary deaths of 70 million people from malaria and other mosquito-borne diseases. This was a genocide policy, a depopulation policy. So, that was 1962.

In 1968, an organization was founded called the Club of Rome, which the LaRouche organization has a great history of denouncing and fighting against. In 1972, the Club of Rome put out a book called *The Limits to Growth*, which we countered with a book called *There Are No Limits to Growth*. In 1982 Helga LaRouche founded the Club of Life in direct opposition to the anti-human outlook of the Club of Rome.

Mass Murder Becomes Policy

In 1991 the Club of Rome issued a book, *The First Global Revolution*, written by Alexander King and Bertrand Schneider, which outrageously puts forth:

Prince Philip wants you to give him a hand.

In searching for a new enemy to unite us, we came up with the idea that pollution, the threat of global warming, water shortages, famine, and the like would fit the bill.... But in designating them as the enemy, we fall into the trap of mistaking symptoms for causes. All these dangers are caused by human intervention, and it is only through changed attitudes and behavior that they can be overcome.... The real enemy, then, is humanity itself.

In 1970, the former Nazi Party member Prince Bernhard helped found the 1001 Club, which was an association of 1001 representatives of the top oligarchical families and moneyed interests. The 1001 Club provided a multimillion-dollar per annum war chest for the WWF, to ensure that the funds would be there to spread this depopulation policy around the world. *This is the process that created and funded the environmentalist movement.* It was entirely—from the beginning—the spawn of the British Royal Family, former Nazis, and top oligarchical families. The year 1970 also saw the first Earth Day, and it was also around this time that it was decided that the last three Apollo missions, Apollo 18, 19, and 20, would be cancelled—and that Apollo 17 in 1972 would be the last time that mankind would walk on the Moon.

In 1974, Henry Kissinger, as Secretary of State, published National Security Study Memorandum 200. NSSM-200 declares:

> The U.S. economy will require large and increasing amounts of minerals from abroad, especially from less developed countries. That fact gives the U.S. enhanced interest in the political, economic, and social stability of the supplying countries. Wherever a lessening of population pressures through reduced birth rates can increase the prospects for such stability, population policy becomes relevant to resource supplies and to the economic interests of the United States....

RDB/ATP/Donald Stampfli

President of the WWF Prince Philip visiting WWF offices in Morge, Switzerland in 1965.

Now this document goes on to name 13 specific countries that are projected to be responsible for 45 percent of the population growth over the next decades, all of whom should be targeted for depopulation; including by policies to reduce birth rates and promote abortions, as well as the deliberate covert diverting of food aid. Around this time, by the mid-1970s, the UN was sponsoring a series of conferences on population.

The World Population Conference held in Bucharest in 1974 became famous. It was headed by gems such as anthropologist Margaret Mead, and it was intervened on by Helga LaRouche, who at the time was Helga Zepp. She challenged the idea that humans are a cancer on the planet, and by putting forward our plan for nuclear power she showed how you could develop the world and support billions and billions of people. Helga was famously chased around the room by Margaret Mead with her big staff!

Genocide by Any Other Name ...

It was this oligarchical process which launched the term "sustainable development." One individual who spoke openly was Paul Ehrlich, who wrote a book called *The Population Bomb*. In that book he advocated using targeted food scarcity as a way of controlling the population. Ehrlich had a protégé named John Holdren. Does anybody remember the name John Holdren? John Holdren was the science advisor to Barack Obama. Another individual from this grouping was John Schellnhuber, who is currently an advisor to the German government on climate matters and energy matters. Schellnhuber was knighted by Queen Elizabeth in 2004 when she visited Berlin. He is also an advisor to the Vatican, and he is responsible for the Satanic papal encyclical that came out in 2015 called *Laudato Sí*, which suggested that human beings are burdening Mother Earth with our activity.

In 2009 at the Copenhagen climate conference, Schellnhuber famously said that we now know for sure that the carrying capacity of the planet,—remember, we were just talking about 100 billion people—and Schellnhuber said the carrying capacity of the planet is now known to be *less than 1 billion people*. So, how do you suggest taking a population of 7.5 billion people and reducing it by 7 billion? How do you do that? How would Bertrand Russell do that?

This is the process, this is the money, and these are the people that produced the IPCC, which was founded in 1988. The goal of the IPCC was to induce nations to sign binding agreements to limit their development, limit the use of their resources, and limit their industrialization based on lies about carbon dioxide and climate change. Since the UN Framework Convention on Climate Change in 1994, which produced the infamous Kyoto Protocol, there have been attempts to force nations to sign binding agreements for these limits—to give up their right to develop—which nations like the United States have refused to sign. That's what this recent IPCC report comes out of, which is a follow-up to the failed 2015 Paris climate meeting, which also failed to get the kind of binding agreements they've been going for two decades now.

When you hear in the media, or you read in a news article that "99 point something percent of scientists agree"; when you see articles that say, as I did the other day, that it's now certain that human beings will make almost all mammalian species go extinct and they won't recover for 3 million years; or, you see these alarmist and emotionally charged reports that we're destroying the planet. *This is not science! This is population control!* This is a dying, desperate empire desperately trying to prevent the end of the colonial system.

No Limits to Human Growth

I want to return to what we heard in what Lyndon LaRouche said, because that is a statement *which is based in science*. We currently have the capability of raising the potential population, the carrying capacity so to speak, of our planet to 100 billion people or more. The reason we can do it is that mankind is not an animal. We have a biological organism that we all ride around in, but we're not animals. Human beings have minds which are capable of inventing creative thoughts, creative hypotheses, generating a new thought which never existed before, some of which are discoveries of real, valid universal principles—discoveries which correspond to the way in which the universe actually works, and which give us power in and over that universe. No animal can do that.

With that in mind, take the issue of resources. The British Empire claim is that resources are limited. Take the computer models which were printed in this ridiculous book, *The Limits to Growth*, which has a bunch of graphs showing how food is going to decline, population is going to go up, pollution is going to go up, and you're all going to die. These computer models linearly extrapolate current conditions—or really, manipulated views of current conditions—to have us believe that we're consuming all the world's resources.

But what is a resource? What defines something as a resource for human civilization? Resources aren't fixed. What was uranium to civilization 300 years ago? Of what use was it? It was a color; it was a very nice yellow color. Resources are only fixed if you fix the level of technology. If you refuse to let society develop to the next level of technology, then yes, resources are fixed. In such a case, we will use up the available resources. Ironically, that's the kind of situation that creates pollution. More pollution has been created by sup-

FIGURE 1

ENERGY DENSITY

How much fuel would it take to meet New York City's electricy requirements for 1 year?*

FUEL SOURCE	TONS
wood	16,000,000
coal	8,000,000
petroleum	5,000,000
uranium† (fission)	55
deuterium-tritium (fusion)	0.7
matter-antimatter	0.003

* based on 2015 consumption, disregarding conversion losses.
† uranium fuel, enriched to 5% U-235.

pressing development. Unimaginable amounts of pollution have been created by *suppressing* development than would have been created by allowing the natural process of progress to take over.

Resources are linked to and defined by what universal principles our minds have access to—what universal principles we are applying in the form of new technologies. This occurs every time the human mind makes a leap in how we think the universe works, how we think it's organized. For example: the revolution which created modern chemistry in the 18th and 19th centuries; the atomic revolution at the end of the 19th and early 20th centuries. *These things define and create a new resource base that didn't exist before. That new resource base never could have been taken into account in any computer model*, even if they were honest. So, we create new resources, we create new things. This succession of resources isn't just replacing one with another. There's actually an ordering principle to it.

So, you see here this chart titled "Energy Density." [**Figure 1**] You see on the left of this table the fuel source—a succession from wood, to coal, to petroleum, to uranium to deuterium and tritium, which are the atomic revolution with fission and fusion. And then to what we think will be matter/anti-matter reactions.

Now, how much fuel would it take to meet New York City's electricity requirements for one year? If all of New York's energy were supplied by burning wood, it would take 16 million tons of wood to meet that requirement every year. If it were supplied by coal, half of

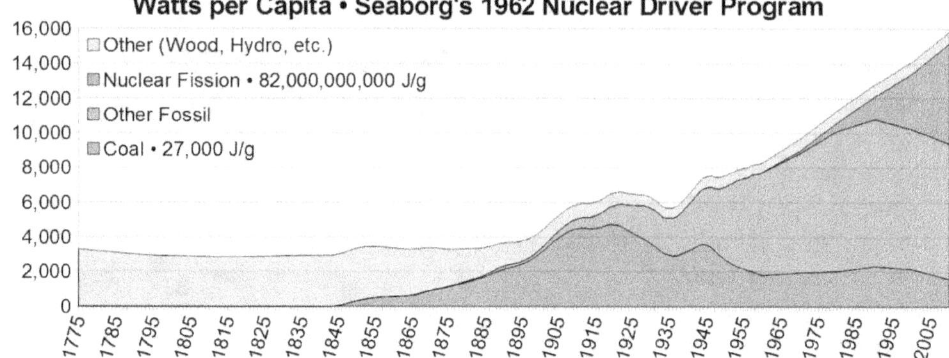

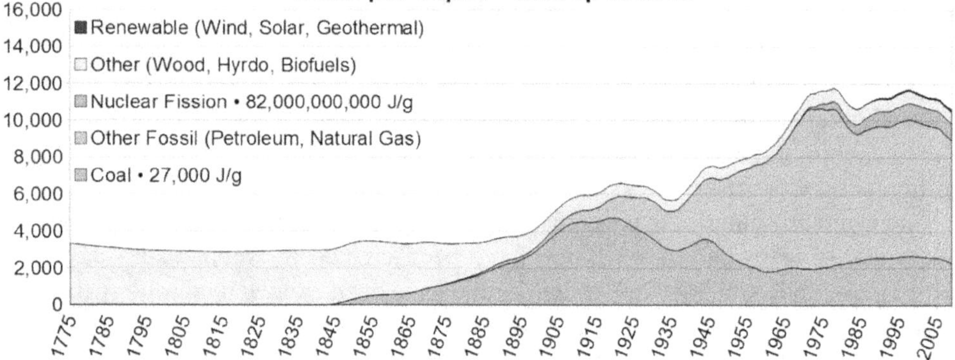

With the kinds of power available to us with the atomic age, we can do other things. We can manipulate the atomic properties of matter, we can create and give matter new properties it didn't have before, like higher degrees of strength, higher degrees of temperature resilience, more flexibility. We can lase light and use light to cut through steel. With plasma processes, we can vaporize any material down to its constituent elements.

What we are talking about, is mankind again and again creating himself on a higher level.

Building for the Future

Just to conclude, I want to take a look at the actual power requirements of the world. We talk a lot about the fact that the world is entering a new paradigm, a post-Empire, post-colonial paradigm. We've been talking for decades about building the World Land-Bridge. What does it mean to build the World Land-Bridge in energy terms? We need to discuss that. We're talking about completely eliminating poverty, relegating that to a phase of the past in mankind's history.

Just to give you a rough idea, if we talk about energy requirements in a relatively developed country such as the United States, we have to look at watts per capita. This is primary energy consumption. This doesn't just mean the electricity you use when you turn on the light switch. This is all of the energy that's required per capita in society, including heating, transportation, energy to move things within the country, to power industries, to power farms, to produce electricity. If you add up the total energy requirements in the United States, and then divide it by the population size to get per capita use, it has been going up since 1775, i.e., since the American Revolution. Each person in the United States has been more and more energy intensive over time, and it's been going up at an accelerating rate.

What you see here, [**Figure 2**] at least as a shadow

that, 8 million tons; by petroleum, 5 million. By uranium, if New York City were nuclear powered, it would take 55 tons of uranium. Fifty-five tons versus 8 million for coal. Fusion? Less than 1 ton.

Each new discovery gives us access to resources which are more powerful, which represent a higher level of power in the universe. It also lets us apply a higher density of power at the point of production, of power applied in industrial and other uses, and this allows us not just to do more, but to do new kinds of things, that would have been impossible before: For example, going to space.

Who thinks we could power a rocket with wood? [laughter] Or with coal? Imagine a guy shoveling coal into the back of the rocket! It's not only a silly idea, it's actually *impossible*. No matter how big a rocket you had, and no matter how many guys you hand on hand to shovel coal, it's physically impossible. A rocket has to carry not only its own weight, but the weight of the fuel that it's burning to get it up there.

But with chemical and then, in the future, nuclear fuel, not only can we get to space, we will be able to accelerate travel speeds to get to Mars in a matter of weeks rather than months.

of a certain technological progress, is that the kind of fuel that's been supplying that energy has been changing. So, we went from being a wood-burning society for about a century, and then we started incorporating coal, which you see really took over as a proportion of the energy fuel supply; then you see we started incorporating oil and natural gas, which led to a huge rise in the energy used per capita. And then, you see this little red sliver up here, the entrance of nuclear power, in the late 1950s/early 1960s. But then, in the 1970s, the power per capita started levelling off. So, the United States has gone *down*. By 2010, the per-capita energy consumption has actually gone down significantly.

To give you a perspective of what *could* have happened, a projection was made during the JFK Administration, which said that if we kept going and incorporated nuclear power, and kept developing our industrial base, we could be going toward 16 kW/capita, *which is about 50 percent higher than where we are today*. So that's going to give you an idea of what a healthy development looked like, at least reflected in energy terms.

Now, let's now think globally: If we suppose that 50 years from now the world population has grown to about 13 billion, let's say, nearly double, so the world has about 13 billion people. If each individual has a living standard, at least reflected in energy terms, comparable to that of the United States today, that would require increasing the energy per capita in the world, from the currently abysmally low 2.5 kW/person average, with many nations below that. The United States is at about 10 kW/person and we should be at about 15 or 20 kW/person. If we were to raise the world average to 13 kW/person, for 13 billion people that would require a *tenfold* increase over where we are today in total world energy consumption.

This would mean that electricity production would not only go up in absolute terms, but should go up as the proportion of energy consumed as electricity, which means you have a lot more industry in your country. We're talking about a *15-fold increase* over the current world levels of electricity consumption. That amounts to the equivalent of building *40,000 new nuclear power plants in the world over the next 50 years*, just to give you some rough numbers. And these are probably low estimates.

That alone, building the equivalent of *40,000* nuclear power plants, is an industrial revolution in and of itself. But we can do that, we absolutely can do that.

Reasserting a Human Identity

Now, the question is: Why should we do that? Come back to LaRouche's idea of 100 billion people. Do we really want that? Do we want 100 billion people on the planet, or more?

Yes, we do. The world is vastly underpopulated.

Man is the only species that can discover universal principles. When we do that, we not only improve the human species, we increase the anti-entropy; we increase the potential for the development of the universe around us. We improve the biosphere far beyond what it could achieve without us. For example, the biosphere cannot travel to the Moon without our species. Human beings can bring life to other planets.

Now, in the next century, the human species will begin to inhabit and do work on other bodies in our Solar system—the Moon and probably Mars, to start. In this process of development, we are going to encounter paradoxes in science that challenge our fundamental beliefs about how the universe works. This is going to require *new* hypotheses, *new* ideas about *new* physical principles that we can't even imagine today, which are going to overturn everything in the way you think the universe works! And these discoveries will give us even higher power in and over nature.

The resource for that kind of unending process of progress, the only *fixed* resource in that, is the human mind. And so, it really is our job now, with the potential of this emerging new paradigm, with this Empire *so exposed* in the fraud of what they've been pushing, and so rejected by the majority of humanity at this point. We have not just a potential but the real responsibility to form a new paradigm of human progress.

And that means we have to create the potential for a lot of geniuses. And that means that we have to create the conditions now, for those geniuses to come into existence. We have to shut down this anti-people, anti-population policy; we have to reject it, and we have to get the United States to join in the intention of what China is leading with the Belt and Road Initiative—*and more than that: the higher vision that the LaRouches have had for decades now, of a real, global Renaissance, the real uniting of mankind around a common mission for our common progress*.

Thank you.

LYNDON H. LAROUCHE, JR, IN 2001

Are You Willing To Make the Change?

Mr. LaRouche addressed the annual conference of the Civil Rights Movement Solidarity party (BüSo) in Mainz, Germany, on Nov. 17, 2001.

We are in a period of history which is unlike anything that, probably, any of you have experienced in your lifetime. And this period of history, which most of you do not know even from studies, this type: It's a period where everything that seemed to be conventional and expected, suddenly vanished. And things came forward, and became dominant, as if from nowhere, at least in the eyes of most people. These are characteric of the truly great revolutionary periods of history, the great upheavals which mark the separation between entire phases of history, sometimes the existence of the nations. We're in such a period.

The reason, why all of these political parties, of the Americas and Western and Central Europe, will soon disappear from the scene, is because they have come from a period which is past, and have entered a shift, into a period in which they are irrelevant.

Now, this is not really something to be described. There's a principle involved. It's a principle which I've sometimes referred to, in writing on the subject of the "goldfish bowl." The way society is organized, is not really rational. It is not, so far. Societies are organized, like the Roman Empire, on a system which has many of the elements of *vox populi*. It's called "popular opinion." Popular opinion varies in its composition, from nation to nation, and time to time. It is generally thought of in terms of the acceptance of certain institutions: institutions of government; institutions of law; institutions of financial and accounting practice; institutions of taste, dress, custom, and expression of opinion. When people wish to influence other people, they will generally appeal to some of these generally accepted institutions, or opinions, as the authority for their behavior. In turn, they believe themselves to be compelled

Lyndon LaRouche addresses the annual conference of the Civil Rights Movement Solidarity party (BüSo). "It's a period of great danger, globally. It's also a period of great opportunity. The question whether the danger will be mastered, will depend upon how many natural, organic leaders, come forth from the population, to exert leadership; leadership of the quality, which Schiller identifies as the Sublime."

to behave as these habits instruct them to behave. And when the time comes that these assumptions of institutions, habits, laws, and so forth, no longer work, then you have the spectacle, which is like the legendary goldfish, which, being released from a bowl into a large pond, swims in small circles, because that is its habit: That is public opinion; that is popular opinion; that is what the Romans called *vox populi*.

What is changed, then, [are] certain assumptions which are—relative to a far more Classical education in geometry, in Euclidean geometry—are changes in axioms or definitions, axioms and postulates, of the way a people and its society think. Now, what if you come to a world, as people did in, for example, 16th-Century Europe? The world of Kepler. And Kepler's accomplishment, in becoming the first founder of a comprehensive mathematical physics, especially with his discoveries in astronomy and astrophysics: What Kepler showed, is that all of his predecessors, including Claudius Ptolemy, Copernicus, and Brahe, were absurd in their fundamental assumptions about the way the universe worked. Because they assumed that the universe would work, according to the kind of lawfulness, which had been prescribed by Aristotle, in his writings. And science showed, as in the case of Kepler—but also in earlier writings of the same type, back to Plato—that this assumption, that a fixed set of generally believed assumptions, was true, was overturned. And this became known as modern science.

Modern science is based, very simply, on the discovery of the absurdity of previously established scientific opinion. And experimental evidence is presented, which presents these scientists with a—let's call it an ontological paradox: a contradiction in physical terms, in which the same standard of mathematical physics, for example, says that something works, but the same, in another experimental case—it doesn't work. And therefore, you have a contradiction between the two cases.

Typical is the case of Fermat, in showing that they had two kinds of phenomena in light, in the bending of light: One, reflection, which appears to follow a pathway of shortest distance. And then, you have another thing: refraction, in which it doesn't. Now, therefore, your concept of time itself, and of the relationship of matter, space, and time, must be radically changed, to take into account the fact of refraction. And much of the work of the 17th Century, of the followers of Fermat, such as Huyghens and Leibniz and Jean Bernoulli, and so forth, was based on the implications of this discovery, that space, time, and matter, as conventionally defined, in that time, were absurd, and the case of refraction proved it. The best accomplishments in modern physics come from that kind of thinking.

So, the way mankind advances—and this is particularly true of modern European civilization: With modern European civilization, and its impact, the rate of increase of the ability of human beings to exist, to

"Thus the legendary goldfish, which continues to swim in small circles...."

increase their life expectancy, to increase the quality of life, had been increased as never before in human existence. This gift of European civilization was created by two things: by the creation of the modern sovereign form of nation-state, the thing that people are now trying to destroy; and by the introduction of science, as a mode of general practice, of general change of practice. This resulted in the greatest increase in the human population ever seen, the greatest rate of increase; the greatest improvement of the potential conditions of life, of life expectancy, and quality of life, intellectually, in all of human existence, for the population as a whole. But it's always based on this principle.

Realize that whatever you believe contains an absurdity. Whatever institutions exist, contain an absurdity. And sooner or later you'll discover what that absurdity is. And the question is posed to you: Are you willing to make the change? Are you will to accept the evidence, the scientific evidence that what you believe is, in part, absurd? That you must concoct an hypothesis, the kind of thing that Kant forbids you to do! But you must test that hypothesis experimentally to determine whether or not it is true. And if it is tested successfully, then you must apply that proven hypothesis to effect a *change* in the behavior in society as well as yourself.

Revive Classical Education

The problem is, that when we come to these changes in political and social institutions, we do not have, any more, a society based on a Classical education, a Classical humanist form of education. The lack of a Classical humanist form of education means that people don't *know* anything; they simply *learn* a great deal. We teach our children the way we teach dogs to do tricks. We do not educate our children to *know*, by *reliving* the great discoveries of the great minds of the past, which you do in a Classical humanist education. We are swayed by popular taste, not by knowledge. We act like trained animals in a circus, or a carnival. We've come to the point that being a trained animal is sometimes fun in a circus, because the animal is fed daily, the tents are put up properly, the care is what they expect. But one day, the circus goes bankrupt, and then, the animals have a terrible time. The same thing happens to society. The "animals" have a terrible time.

But, because we do not have a society that is educated in science, in the scientific way of thinking, as Kepler, Leibniz, and so forth; because we have a society in which Classical humanist education has been banned, for example, in Germany, for the past 30 years. Therefore, you have, among Germans, for example: You meet a German who was educated in the Classical humanist education, the Humboldt system, *prior* to the Brandt reforms, and one who was educated *after* the Brandt reforms: it's like meeting *two different species.* One inferior, morally, to the other. The ability to think is lacking, has been largely destroyed. We have in the labor force in the United States, we have not only vast unemployment, in fact, but we have people who are un-qualified for work. We have people who are not quali-fied for the kinds of jobs which have disappeared, which are the jobs they used to be trained for, but which no longer exist, at least not in great numbers.

So, we've come to a point, in which we have to make a change. The existing parties are based, and base their success, on the record of success in influencing institutions, under conditions which *no longer exist.* And by their clinging to the anchor of a sinking ship for security, *they drown in their own folly.*

So, our problem is to understand this process, and understand that, in dealing with people throughout the world, we have to deal with this problem. We're dealing with people who *don't know how to think.* They have been taught *to learn, not to know.* There-fore, politics, real politics today, takes the form of *applied Classical humanist education*, of thinking, pre-paring, when you're dealing with people, to present what they need to know, in the form of the experienc-ing of an ontological paradox, a relevant ontological paradox, and working through the process of discov-ery, to see what the principle is, which that paradox requires us to discover. And when they have shared the discovery of that principle, *then they know it.*

So, being in real politics today, is actually a form of *applied Classical humanist education*: in science, in emphasis on Classical poetry, Classical drama. Because the only way you can transform society from one that doesn't work, like the present European nations, or the present United States, is by educating the population to *know.* How can a population have the confidence to make revolutionary changes, suddenly, and in large numbers, if they don't *know* what they're doing? They can continue to stumble into the ditch by following the habits they've acquired, habits expressed by the exist-ing political parties, which might be called the rubbish dump of dead ideas. You have a dead idea, you jump into one of these rubbish dumps, and you are disposed of in due course. But, if you want to be a part, a relevant part of the conditions of life which are emerging, then, you have to know what you're doing. To influence large numbers of people, to make a fundamental change in the way *they* behave, they have to know what they're doing. And therefore, the issue is that.

How an Economy Functions

Let me just give one example of this from my own personal standpoint: Some years ago, now, over 50 years ago, I made a certain series of scientific discover-ies, in the field of physical economy. These were made in the course of refuting the absurdity of the arguments for information theory by Norbert Wiener, and the argu-ments for systems analysis and artificial intelligence by John von Neumann, both of whom were acolytes, in their childhood or youth, of Bertrand Russell, and who represented a principle of pure evil. But, later, in the course of working through these discoveries I made, I found, I turned again to Bernard Riemann, and found out what kind of a conception you had to have—how do you organize such a set of ideas into a functioning econ-omy? And therefore, the ideas of Riemann became an integral part of my own discoveries.

In the course of this, I came to understand how modern economies function. They function in terms of long waves, long cycles, not the way Kondratieff de-scribed it for the Russians, but another kind of long cycle. The cycles are, as Kondratieff suggested, largely technologically based. That is, when a society has ad-opted a certain kind of general technology, that technol-ogy, as the population becomes more proficient in it, as investment occurs, that wave of technology will tend to result in an increase in the productive powers of labor, and other benefits. After a while, not making additional new discoveries will result in the same society, which succeeded in that wave of technology, will then go into an attritional period of decline.

So we have these characteristic cycles in society, which are largely cycles of ideas; in physical science, they're cycles of physical ideas, or how to apply them. There are also cycles in the way people cooperate. If you educate people in the Classical humanist mode, in an educational system, then you will have a labor force which is able to think, which knows. Such a labor force can more rapidly assimilate new technologies; whereas a labor force which is trained like a donkey to pull the same load, given a different job to do, can't do it. So, you have cycles of culture, as well as physical science, as such.

Thus, in analyzing economies, I always look at this question of axiomatics. What are the principles which cause an economy to behave the way it does? We say an economy is behaving the way it does because the people in it, the form of government institutions, the form of laws, the form of accounting procedures, and other customs, caused that society to behave in a certain way, as if it were a very specific kind of geometry, in which nothing can happen that doesn't fit the assumptions, the definitions, axioms, and postulates of that geometry.

And therefore, a society has a cyclical characteristic; the most typical cycle is that of one generation, or two generations. If you look at the history of economy, the history of events, you find that the period from the age of birth, to the age of about 25 years, is a characteristic cycle in modern society, because it takes about 25 years to take a child, and bring it to maturity as a professional in modern society. But, you will find that, for example, investments in infrastructure—benefits last for a quarter-century to a half-century. There are investments that take that long. Investment in an agricultural program by a farmer: He has to plant a crop program, he has to develop the crop program, which in vegetable crops is lower; if he has to develop cattle, like high-quality dairy cattle, it may take 25 years to build up a decent herd of high-quality dairy cattle. It's not done so easily, so it's an investment over a period of time, whose fruit is harvested over a period of time, and which is used up over a period of time.

And so, we think about 5-year cycles; not so much, but 10-, 20-year, 50-year cycles are the kind of cycles we experience in physical economy. And political economy tends to follow underneath the needs and impact of physical economy.

The Post-War Policy Crisis

And the problem has been, that, in the postwar period, since 1945, the policies which the United States had intended to follow had Roosevelt lived, were not carried out. Those policies meant the immediate elimination of colonialism, immediate! That the French, the British, the Dutch, the Portuguese colonies would be instantly wiped from the map, as colonies, and independent nations would stand where colonies had stood the moment before. The United States, which had built up a large war machine, an industrial war machine, intended to *convert* that industrial war machine into a production machine for capital goods, for the world at large. In conjunction with developing, as Roosevelt laid out in a famous meeting he had in Casablanca, in 1942, to develop Africa, Asia, areas of colonialism as independent nations, and the United States, while helping Europe to recover from the combined effects of depression and war, would also devote a large part of its production to meeting the needs of what we call today, developing nations. We didn't do that.

We didn't do that.

But we developed a Bretton Woods system of modified form, which, unfortunately, was based on an artificial conflict between the Soviet system and the Anglo-American system. We lived on this mixture of conflict, and a fairly good economic system for Western Europe, Japan, the United States, the Americas, for a period up until the middle of the 1960s.

Then, shortly after the death of Kennedy—the assassination of Kennedy—it was torn down. It was signalled by the ouster of Erhard, here in Germany, which was a turning point downward for the German economy, and the attempt to ruin de Gaulle, in the same period, which was a downturn for the French economy. You will find that most of the benefits, in Germany, that are being taken away today, were those that were built up and set into motion, as part of the postwar economic recovery, from 1945 through the middle of the 1960s. You find the same thing in France; France is living on the fag-end of the exhaustion of what Charles de Gaulle, as President, contributed to the development of France, essentially.

The same thing is true around the world. The United States, Western Europe, Japan, and most of the Americas, increased their productivity, improved their standard of living, improved the conditions of life, consistently, over about that period, from 1945 to 1964-65. That was a cycle.

Then there were the changes that came, coinciding with the war in Vietnam. There were the radical changes, in culture, in politics, and in economics. And from 1965 on, Europe and the United States *willfully* began to *to destroy its own economy,* its own productive capability. Just make a list! Of the great German firms, for example. Industrial firms, which existed, employed people and so forth, in 1965. Make a list of those, which have disappeared, or have shrunken into obscurity, since that time.

There's another cycle: Over the past 35 years, the world system, the so-called Anglo-American system, has been dominated by this degeneration. This degeneration was accelerated, by the collapse of Soviet system. With the collapse of the Soviet system, Anglo-American interests believed that they had established a potential world empire, like the Roman Empire; or more like a Venetian model of the Roman Empire, that is, where a rentier-financier group of parasites would run the world, from the standpoint of their financial interests. Nation-states, as such, would be destroyed, as was done with the Maastricht treaties—these kinds of things. This process of *destruction* of civilization, *accelerated* after 1989! It shouldn't have! The right policy could have been followed. It wasn't.

The policy was, to *take the opportunity of the collapse of the Soviet adversarial posture, as an excuse for accelerating the rate of destruction of economy!* Which is what happened.

We've now come to the point, that that system, for its own *axiomatic reasons, is finished! It's over!* We are now standing at the *end-phase* of an entire period of history! The end-phase of, actually, the entire 1945 to 2001 interval of history, which contains within it several cycles. And, by looking at the assumptions of policy-making, the assumption of prevailing ideas, which have guided of each of these changes, I was able to make forecasts, which have been, on record now, the most accurate long-range economic forecasts made by anyone in the entire past 55-60 years. Simply because I emphasized what I had discovered: that you do not look, from week to week, from month to month, from statistics, and try to determine where an economy is going. You look at the *underlying, axiomatic assumptions, that control the behavior, of populations and their component parts.* And, thus you can foresee, if you think ahead.

Lessons of Classical Tragedy

The problem we have—another one, the crucial one, which I'm sure Helga [Zepp LaRouche] referred to today, because I know she was going to do something like that—is the question of the Sublime.

The greatest problem we have today, is not just the problems I've discussed, but something related to that: that tragedy, as I'm sure Helga emphasized, does not lie in a mis-leader. Tragedy lies in a bad people, with a bad culture. The great figures of tragedy—the leading figures of tragedy—were bad because they were *consistent,* in their behavior and outlook, with the society which they led. What was bad, was the lack of a leader, who would *lead the society away* from its habits. In each case of a tragedy—and remember, all the great Classical tragedies were based either on actual history, or upon legends, which had a historical significance, such as those of the Homeric epics. So, in all real Classical tragedy, the writer was writing about real events, with the skill of a tragedian, and we should study these things to see how the mind of the great Classical tragedians worked, in understanding the critical points, by which a people of a culture *destroyed themselves.* It was not a mis-leader: It was *they,* themselves, that destroyed themselves. As civilization today is destroying itself; as Western Europe is destroying itself; as the United States is destroying itself. It is not being destroyed from the outside: It's being destroyed *inside, by its own people! By its own culture!* Why? Because it has the willpower, to be able to make decisions which would change it: *But they don't make the changes.* It is that characteristic behavior, of not *making* the changes in a timely fashion, which is the force of tragedy, in real history, as we face it today.

Moral Requirements for Leadership

So, therefore, what's the problem? The problem we face—when you get into a situation like mine, you face it more clearly, than, perhaps, in any other position. In a position, where you have some leadership, some influence, of things in the world, on a fairly significant scale sometimes. And, you know how to solve the problem that threatens civilization. But, you find the institutions and people aren't willing to do it. They are, in a sense, *not willing to survive,* if it means giving up a set of definitions, axioms, and postulates, that govern their behavior. That's how societies are doomed. Not making a breakthrough, to freedom.

And, thus, the problem is: How do we understand

this problem? We say, "Forget this business about, 'the people are good.'" Well, every human being is born good. That is, they have the creative power, which is goodness. The job is, to develop it; to bring it to fruition; to make it efficient. But most people never mature. Even people,— often scientists: They never mature. They remain bad children. Their sense of identity is located in a very small geographic area, in a relatively small set of social relations. Within a short term of time, when you look at things like the great figures of tragedy—the ones who are not tragic in themselves—the great figures often sacrificed their lives, not as a human sacrifice, but by putting their lives at risk, by doing what they knew to be necessary, to lead their society out of the grip of a tragedy.

"Great leaders inspire a population to rise above its pettiness." Germany's Chancellor Konrad Adenauer (left) and France's President Charles de Gaulle.

The problem is, there are very few people today, who have that moral quality. There have been relatively few people in all history, who've had that quality, to rise above the littleness, the mediocrity, the small-mindedness, the petty self-interest of the average person. People say, "If you're so smart, why aren't you successful?" "Why would you do that? You would ruin your career!" And, it's by that kind of small-mindedness, that people in positions of power become *fools*, by trying to be realistic and successful.

Whereas, the hero, the true hero, who typifies what is called the Sublime in Classical art, is the person, who knows the change that has to be made, in the assumptions of the society, to save the society, *and will risk everything, as necessary, to bring about that change.*

The only thing that saves a people, from the kind of self-destruction, which European nations and the United States are bringing upon themselves today, is to find among them *leaders*, who will represent the Sublime, who will do what *is necessary*, for the nation, for the people, and for the future, whatever the risk that entails for themselves.

And, people are not stupid. Even when they're behaving badly. We find that you can often, if you have those qualities, you can often *touch them* in people. Great leaders inspire a population *to rise above its pettiness.* For example, as de Gaulle did. De Gaulle was the leader of France. He came to France, and they struggled against a coup d'état, against him, and an earlier coup. He gave a famous speech, which I saw on television, and he said to the French population: *"Aidez moi"* [help me]. And, the French population responded, and France was saved. De Gaulle, the hero, in that moment, who *saved* France, and saved Europe from the hell which would have resulted, had he not succeeded!

It is *always* that. When you look at the history of the rise of Nazism in Germany: *There were people on the scene, who could have prevented that! And, didn't.* Because, they wanted to work within the system, to control the problem. The same thing is true, in all history. There have always been people, on the scene—to my knowledge—who had the knowledge, and had the impulse in the right direction, to provide leadership. But that leadership was often rejected. Or, they didn't cultivate their powers of leadership, adequately. Didn't rely upon it. They flinched. They vacillated. And, therefore, a nation was lost, or went to hell.

We're in such a period, now. So, I think it's a period of great danger, globally. It's also a period of great opportunity. The question whether the danger will be mastered, will depend upon how many natural, organic leaders, come forth from the population, to exert leadership; leadership of the quality, which Schiller identifies as the Sublime.

Thank you.